"God has a unique design and destiny for [...] ognize what our purpose is because we're s[...] Tim Waisanen has worked with young people for years. He understands the stage of life they're in—and it's a critical stage in terms of discovering purpose. *The Purpose Experience* provides hands-on strategies, inspiring stories, and biblical truths to empower you to realize the unique, one-of-a-kind calling that God has for YOU!"

—Martijn van Tilborgh, Author, speaker, and entrepreneur

"AT LAST, a solid, practical solution for all who are just wandering through life. 'Let no man despise your youth. . .' the apostle Paul writes to Timothy. Now, two thousand years later, Tim Waisanen writes this instruction manual on how to accomplish that. In fact, a person can have a healthy pride about who they are and what they do, and others will feel that way about them too. For more than a decade, Tim and I have talked and prayed together. His passion and excitement are deep and real. His writing is much more than philosophical research; he has lived the experience of being salvaged from the hopeless dead ends of a wandering life, and moving into a life of accomplishment, fulfillment, happiness, and peace. He is the 'real deal.' The evidence is in the fruit of his labors: literally thousands of youth on several continents rescued from their meaningless wanderings and despair. If you know in your deepest thoughts that 'There must be more to life than this,' then don't think twice about getting *The Purpose Experience*. Read it slowly. Highlight it. Take it in. You have nothing to lose and a lot to gain."

—Nelson R. Alsup
Director, The Way Up Christian Counseling
Orlando, Florida

"*The Purpose Experience* is a trend-setting book that will greatly impact whomever reads it! Tim's real-life, riveting personal stories, along with paradigm-breaking purpose principles, will ignite the passion in everyone to live differently! This book is on the cutting-edge for those who want to make a difference with their lives!"

—Mark Schrade
Senior Pastor, City Sanctuary Church
Deland, Florida

"Tim is one of the best leaders I have ever seen at raising up healthy young leaders and disciples of Christ in my over thirty years of ministry. He uses time-tested "purpose principles" that are a key part of this process, and I am thrilled to see they are now available for everyone. They are practically implemented in a clear way and will become an effective guide to help those seeking to discover and grow in their purpose."

—PASTOR JEFF KRALL
One Lord One Body Ministries

"In *The Purpose Experience*, Tim Waisanen brings not only a practical approach to helping anyone find their purpose, but he also brings a lifetime of experience, not just theory. There is no better person in the world to bring the message in this book. I truly hope you won't miss the opportunity to dig in and get started on finding God's purpose for your life. This is the guide you've been looking for!"

—NICK NANTON, ESQ.
Emmy Award-Winning Movie Director/Producer
Agent to Celebrity Experts

"Nothing has the power to energize and inspire like knowing why you were born! Understanding this determines whether you succeed or fail in life and is the standard by which all your endeavors are to be measured. In *The Purpose Experience,* Tim Waisanen beautifully unlocks the roadmap to this exciting journey of self-discovery and revelation. From beginning to end, Tim challenges you to go deeper, to grapple with the real issues of life, and to take hold of that for which you were born. *The Purpose Experience* will help you find and unlock the life you were made for! I heartily recommend it!"

—PASTOR RON JOHNSON
One Church
Orlando, Florida

"*The Purpose Experience* is an exceptional narrative work which distinctively captures and answers pressing questions experienced by individuals within our present society. Tim Waisanen, through this engaging piece, is able to bring insight into what it means to actually understand and walk in God's full purpose for your life.

In this era of discovery, Tim has dedicated himself to enlightening the pursuit of our younger generation. Purpose, self-discovery, and destiny are all key frameworks which Tim has done an excellent job discussing. *The Purpose Experience* is truly an impactful book which creates a sense of awakening and pursuit towards God's original plan and framework for our lives. It will be a blessing to all who read it. Keep up the wonderful work."

—Dr. Forson Swanzy
Pastor, Forerunners Generation International
Spiritual advisor to CEOs and former NFL players

"*The Purpose Experience* is a profoundly impactful resource, not just because its truth is timeless and biblical, but because its truth has been lived out in the twenty years I've known Tim. His passion is discipling young leaders, helping them to discover and live out their purpose. I know of few who are as committed to relational disciple-making as Tim."

—Doug Holliday
Executive Director, Sonlife Ministries
sonlife.com

"As the director of an organization that serves US military stationed around the world, we have been honored to work with Tim Waisanen and the People of Purpose team for the past ten years in six nations: Germany, Belgium, Italy, Japan, S. Korea and the USA. The quality of ministry, as well as the dedication to the vision of helping individuals find their God-ordained purpose in life, is unparalleled. Tim has prepared this writing not just out of intensive prayer and study but out of real-life experience around the world. I am sure this book will be a blessing and bear fruit for everyone who receives its valuable input. Whether you serve the Lord around the corner or around the globe, may this resource both equip and inspire you to make an eternally-impacting difference in the world."

—Jennie Humann
International Director, Jacob's Generation
The Children, Youth, and Families of Freedom Outreach International
JacobsGen.org, MTTM.org

"I'm honored and grateful to know Tim as a personal friend, a co-laborer, and a mentor to myself and my family. Tim's caring, humorous, patient, and graceful approach to changing lives is second to only One. I've watched him connect with young people and lead them into their purposes for two decades. The fruit of their lives can be traced back to their relationship with God and the man who led them to the Lord in the first place. *The Purpose Experience* is a toolbox of spiritual practices and practical application. It's truly a guide for all of us to lead generations into their purpose and calling."

—DON CAMPBELL
Founder, Feeding Children Everywhere
Business and Nonprofit Consultant

"*The Purpose Experience* could only have been written by a person who has experienced the purpose of existence. God has mentored Tim Waisanen through many life experiences of family, friends, and others who have been placed in his journey of life. Tim has a profound love for young people in their teens and early adulthood; that is what makes what he says valid to those who read and hear his words of wisdom and experience. Every person who reads this book will benefit from its contents, strengthening their journey of life and purpose."

—DR. A. JOHN MURPHY, JR.
Founder, Harvest Time International

"Shalom to all youth pastors, youth Bible study teachers, and college-aged young adults. I personally have known Tim for many years as a man after and always interested in God's own heart, with a desire to share these timeless fragments of information from the Hebrew perspective of the Scriptures. He and I have shared countless hours navigating through many of the most intriguing topics all with one goal in mind: to share this wealth of information with you! I highly recommend *The Purpose Experience* to all those desiring to expand the knowledge they already have and acquire new insights as never before. May the Eternal God of Israel richly bless you in all you do."

—RABBI GARY FERNANDEZ
Head Rabbi, Synagogue Beth Israel
Sanford, Florida

THE
PURPOSE
EXPERIENCE

DISCOVER AND FULFILL YOUR
GOD-GIVEN PURPOSE

TIM WAISANEN

THE PURPOSE EXPERIENCE ⊘

ARROWS &
STONES

For foreign and subsidiary rights, contact the author.

Cover design by Sara Young
Cover author's photo by Andrew van Tilborgh

ISBN: 978-1-954089-13-6   1 2 3 4 5 6 7 8 9 10

Printed in the United States of America

DEDICATIONS

To my amazing and supportive wife, Karla. If it weren't for you, this book would never have been written. Your belief in me, prayers for me, and continuous sacrifice have given me fuel and the freedom to live out my purpose. Our joint surrender to the call of God and living out these purpose principles have been the breeding ground and catalyst to birth this purpose message. Very few truly know the heavy price we have paid together to pursue God's call upon our lives. Thank you for loving me and standing by me through the lowest valleys and highest mountain-tops as we have pursued Jesus together around the world! Your incredibly positive attitude and love for Jesus is contagious, and it has breathed life into me during the toughest times when I have wanted to quit. I love you and am forever grateful. This book is filled with our story and our life's work together up to this point as our story is still being written. I believe millions of souls will find purpose and be in heaven as a result. You have helped make me a better, godly man, husband, father, and leader. You are my best friend, and I love you with all my heart and soul!

To my son, Elisha, and daughter, Debi. I wrote this book for you. This is my life's story and unfiltered truth of God's redemption purpose in my life. I pray this will be a tool and road map to guide you into living out your purpose. May it be a constant reminder of God's faithfulness and promises as you bring the message of purpose through Jesus to this lost world. May you build upon these principles and soar even higher than your mom and me. Our ceiling is your floor. Use your amazing gifts for the glory of God to change your generation! Nobody believes in you more than I do. Being your dad is one of my greatest privileges on this earth, and your lives bring so much laughter and joy! I love you both!

To my family. My greatest cheerleaders, prayer warriors, and inspiration. Without you all, I wouldn't be in ministry, be who I am today, or have the confidence to do what I do. You have taught me to chase God's dreams with unshakable faith. You have sacrificially given up your time, energy, and finances to this cause. You are my rock and my safe place, the ones I can always trust and confide in. You all bring me such joy and laughter. I am so thankful to God for your role in my life.

To all my sponsors and close friends. Your continual support, prayers, and belief in me give me the courage to continue the mission. They cause me to believe in myself and remind me we are not alone in this. Together, we are marking a generation of youth with the message of purpose. Your faithfulness and sacrifice to God's work have kept me on the front lines of investing in the next generation. Tens of thousands of souls have been impacted because of your involvement in the kingdom of God through People of Purpose. You share equally in these stories, and may the Lord reward you for all your sacrifice. Thank you for standing with and believing in us!

To my spiritual sons and daughters (there are too many to name). You each hold an extra special place in my heart. You all helped to forge these purpose principles in the fires of ministry over the years as you allowed me access to your lives. Through our relationships, you have helped me become a better leader and blessed me with the opportunity to discover what true biblical discipleship looks like. Watching you all passionately pursue your purpose with faith makes it all worth it and is the only reward I need! You all are the first-fruits of my life's work and living proof these principles work. My prayer is that Karla and I have modeled what lives surrendered to God's purpose look like and that it inspires you to chase after God's purpose for your life. May this book be a resource for you to take and help your spiritual sons/daughters go do the same. I am always here for you—your greatest fan and cheerleader—I am your purpose pastor. You are family to me, and I love you all.

Lastly, to all my mentors (you know who you are). Thank you for all the encouragement and belief in the call of God on my life. I would not be who I am today without your influence! Thank you for the years of guidance and listening to me "think out loud" during the tough seasons as I tried to discern the Lord's direction for my life. Thank you for challenging me to not settle in life and to be the best version of myself. Your voice and wisdom have helped provide inspiration and confidence in what God has called me to do. Some of you have been with me since the day I was born, others came into my life as I was growing up, and others have come alongside me in my adult ministry years. To each of you, I honor you and the gift on your life as each of you has contributed in different ways to my life's purpose. Thank you for investing in me!

CONTENTS

INTRODUCTION

I wrote this book because, after college, I didn't know what to do with my life. I was lost, confused, and overwhelmed. It seemed nobody had answers to my deepest questions. I couldn't see a way out—and this confusion sent me down a deep, dark path that took me years to exit. I had no idea what my purpose was, and after a several-years-long journey of discovering it, I found life-changing keys I would have paid any amount of money to have had back in my twenties. I want to impart these to you. I want to be an empowering guide who not only helps you to discover your purpose but who also helps you live your best life ever!

I wrote this book for every teenager, college student, young adult, or human being asking him or herself , *What is my purpose? Why do I exist? What am I supposed to do with my life? How do I figure out my future?* This book is for those who feel stuck, lost, broken, or unsure about their purpose. It is for those whose hearts cry out that there has to be more than *this*. If you're craving adventure, if you're bored with Christianity as you know it, or **if you yearn for the inner peace that comes from knowing exactly why you were created, this book is for you.** The premise of this book is that you do not find purpose through knowledge alone or by reading about it in a book. You have to experience purpose. These experiences will cause you to live differently, leading to a life of purpose. Come and experience the meaning behind your life's journey.

The truth is that this generation needs to find purpose. I want you to visualize the following facts: The next time you walk into a public place—say, Starbucks—look around. One in seven young adults will need substance abuse treatment at some point. One out of ten are thinking of ending their lives. In fact, 648,000 young people each year attempt suicide![1]

I will never forget the afternoon, one summer day before my sophomore year in high school, when my brother, sister, and I came inside from playing. Our parents said, "Kids, we need you to sit down and have an important conversation with us." Then came the words I never thought I would hear from their mouths. They came out like a tsunami crashing upon an unsuspecting, sleeping village: "We're getting a divorce."

I couldn't believe my ears. I felt like I was dreaming—having an out-of-body experience. I mean, my parents were the last people I ever expected to divorce. They'd been pastors and married for nineteen years. Yet here we sat, listening to them explain the inevitable. This was the moment my life changed forever; it put me on a trajectory that shaped who I have become today. My life was great before the divorce, but after the devastating news, things began to shift. A happy, full-of-life teenager became lost, hurt, angry, and confused. Sometimes, I was fine, but when my thoughts and emotions started to wander, all these feelings would come rolling in. It wasn't long before I started drinking occasionally and pursuing girls in a new way. Not too long after my parents divorced, I lost my virginity and had other sexual encounters that were out-of-character for me.

All the while, my dad would occasionally ask me, "Son, how are you doing? Would you like to see a counselor?"

I'd tell him, "I'm okay, Dad. I'm working through it."

Inside, however, I was deeply hurt, trying to make sense of something impossible to make sense of. I'd become a master at hiding things. Like many of you reading this, I was good at wearing a mask and pretending everything was fine when it wasn't. **I built a complex defense mechanism comprised of self-protection and self-sufficiency that kept others from penetrating my facade.**

---

1 Substance Abuse and Mental Health Services Administration. (2018). Key substance use and mental health indicators in the United States: Results from the 2017 National Survey on Drug Use and Health (HHS Publication No. SMA 18-5068, NSDUH Series H-53). Rockville, MD: Center for Behavioral Health Statistics and Quality, Substance Abuse and Mental Health Services Administration. Retrieved from *https://www.samhsa.gov/data/.*

I made the Florida State Olympic Development Team as a junior in high school, which meant I was one of the best eighteen soccer players in the state of Florida. This opportunity allowed me to be noticed by college coaches and led to God's provision for my education. After I graduated high school, I went to Rollins College in the Orlando, Florida, area on a full soccer scholarship: tuition, room, and board were all paid for! Everything was covered except for my textbooks. Even through my brokenness, God was still providing for me.

During my college years, I joined a fraternity. I had a girlfriend throughout my sophomore and senior years. My prospects were promising, but let's suffice it to say that this chapter wasn't my brightest. I began to drink more. I smoked marijuana multiple times. I became sexually promiscuous. I had begun looking at pornography during high school, but in college, my appetite for it grew. I remember getting drunk on Saturday nights and going to church the next morning and praying to God that my dad wouldn't smell the alcohol on my breath. You see, I still believed in Jesus—and still loved him—but I *hated* the church. I hated what it had done to my family—the gossip, how people had turned their backs on us after my parents had been there for them in their roughest seasons. My parents were human beings, trying to be led by God to help others; now, who was there to help *them*?

None of the partying, sex, marijuana, or friends brought me any lasting joy or calmed the storms inside. I felt devastatingly empty and alone, even though I was constantly surrounded by people. I majored in psychology, as I was fascinated by the reasons people act the way they do. I had no idea about the path God was leading me down (which I will share more about later).

After college, I was ready to take the world by the tail. After all, every graduation speech says that "The world is your oyster," right? You throw your cap with the assumption that life is going to pan out the exact way you plan. Ha! At first, things seemed great. I lived out a childhood dream by playing professional soccer for both the indoor and outdoor teams of the Orlando Lions. During my second year, I sustained a severe ankle injury that caused me to lose motivation. This was a turning point. Again, I continued down that dark path—this time, the despair lasted several years. I tried to suppress my emotional storm in many ways. Drinking and sex became occasional but regular escapes. One of my main coping mechanisms was immersing myself in surfing and soccer as much as possible. This, at least, gave me a sense of focus and fun. Sports helped me block out the problems in my life and made everything temporarily seem all right. However, the emotional high, the adrenaline rush, and the dopamine drip in my brain wore off every time—and nothing had truly changed.

I began to ask myself the questions I know you may be asking yourself right now: *What is my purpose? What is the meaning of my life? What am I going to do in the future?* At a loss, I joined a few different multi-level marketing companies—you know, that kind where you call all your friends and tell them, "Hey! I have a great business opportunity for you!" I ended up $13,000 in credit card debt and more bewildered than ever. So, I did what any college-educated, broke young adult would do: I became a valet at Disney hotels, parking cars. I worked with eighteen year olds for five years in my twenties—clearly, I was using my education well! I tried out every career path I could think of: trading stocks, selling insurance, waiting tables. Nothing seemed to work. Nothing brought fulfillment. Every one brought me to yet another dead end, and I was miserable.

This went on for several years. During this post-grad period, my dad, who was still pastoring, would continue to ask me to consider working at our church. He would say, "Tim, why don't you pray about working with our teenagers?"

I would say, "Okay, Dad. I'll pray about it," go pray, and then come back and say, "Dad, God says no." At one point, I even told him, "Dad, I'll *never* work with teenagers! They're a bunch of punks. I can't stand them!"

He was persistent, though. "Son, I feel like God has a calling on your life to work with young people." Solely because I still had a close relationship with my dad and trusted him, I continued to stay open to his advice.

I had now been in a relationship for six-and-a-half years; we had even been engaged for two years. However, I had never actually set a wedding date. Although my fiancée was a Christian, ours was an unhealthy, sexually-impure relationship. Obviously, I was unsure if she was the one. I strung her along for years during my confusion, and I take full responsibility for my cowardly behavior. I was broken, and she met needs inside of me that my soul desperately craved. I remember asking God, *How did I get here, and how do I get out of this hole?*

Things got exceptionally bad a few times during this period. I was so frustrated and angry that, at times, I wanted to commit suicide. I remember driving home drunk after partying in downtown Orlando. As I sped down the interstate, feeling that same tsunami of emotions collapsing upon my chest, I came close to ramming my car into a telephone pole at seventy miles per hour. I remember one time, specifically, that I was ready to veer off the road. Instead, I quickly pulled over and burst into tears. Looking into the mirror, I yelled, "Tim, what is *wrong* with you? You know better than this! Get it together." I wasn't like this all the time—just in a few key moments when something triggered my feelings of rejection, anger, or hopelessness.

Finally, things came to a head. My stock-trading job ended. I totaled my car. I had to liquidate my mutual fund to pay bills. I went broke. I had nothing. Now, I began to cry out to God and say, "God, I will go anywhere you want me to go. I will do whatever you want me to do. If you want me to be a missionary in India and preach the gospel overseas, I'll go. I'm so miserable. Just *tell me what to do!*"

I prayed this prayer for about six months; finally, one morning, at a hotel in Orlando, God answered me. I was attending a ministry prayer breakfast when He spoke to my heart and said, "Son, I've called you to work with young people. Will you answer the call?" I came home to my apartment. My then-fiancée was still asleep, half-naked, in my bed from the night before. I stood there and whispered to myself, *Tim, you're in deep $&#!* Shortly after that morning, we broke up—this time for good. **A line was drawn in the sand for me. Everything changed. I stepped into the uncertainty of saying yes to what God wanted, instead of my own desires.** I said yes to becoming my dad's youth pastor.

My journey in ministry began in 2001. My first ministry event consisted of me and one eighth grader shooting basketball, playing PIG. Over time, this transformed into hundreds of kids coming to Christ and pursuing their purposes. Today, this adventure has taken me all over the world, to places like Germany, Belgium, Italy, South Korea, Okinawa, El Salvador, Guatemala, Nicaragua, Bolivia, and across America. From preaching on TV, to visiting the poorest villages in Central America, to walking on United States military bases around the world, the journey has been indescribable. We have seen thousands come to Christ, and we've helped launch hundreds of young leaders into their purposes. Through it all, God has shown me key principles of purpose that, when implemented, help people get unstuck and unlock the hidden potential within themselves!

This is not a 100 percent comprehensive plan for purpose. It's a culmination of a thirty-year process I went through in my own journey. This book is raw and unfiltered. The main illustrations used throughout it are from my life. Following the principles we'll explore has unleashed thousands of young adults into their destinies! While this book is written for young adults, the principles are timeless and cross over to all generations. This is a practical road map—a template to follow that will help you both right now as well as in every season of life. If you feel stuck, frustrated, confused, and overwhelmed, this book is for you. If you are uncertain about what path to take, this book is for you. If you've ever wondered, *How do I discover my purpose/direction/college/major/career path?* this book is for you. Come on this journey with me, and discover the best life that God has for you—the life you were created to live!

When I Googled books on "purpose," 811,000 results came up. A general search about purpose yielded 4,080,000 results. I am sure, by now, the number is higher and counting. However, I don't know of anyone who is explaining how to find your purpose *and making it practical.* I want to be your tour guide, not your travel agent. I want to walk with you through this journey instead of just telling you places to visit along the way. I want to make it clear *how* to do it, not just *what* you should do. This book is a road map with which to navigate this season of your life.

A word of warning, however: This journey is not for the faint of heart. It's only for those who are truly hungry for change—and willing to follow these principles. By doing so, you will discover the *very reason you exist.* You will be challenged. Your thinking will be stretched. The truths you discover may even be counterintuitive to your current belief system. **If you aren't satisfied with what you've gotten out of life so far, you have to do something different.** It's time to live your greatest adventure. You were made for more. It's time to be free—to become all you were created to be. Make your life count for something, and leave a legacy that lasts for eternity.

I knew there was more for me—that I wasn't destined for failure, but something had to change. It wasn't until I discovered these critical principles that I was able to break free from what was holding me back, find my purpose, and step into it.

We've helped hundreds of high schoolers, college kids, and twenty-somethings find breakthrough in their lives and live out their purposes. Now, it's your turn. If you're ready to get unstuck, and you're hungry for life to change, then keep reading. This book and the curriculum that guides you through the process afterwards are not just about giving you information; they're about self-discovery and revelation that lead to transformation from the inside out. It's a process that will make those things that were once hidden become clear. Isn't that what you've been craving—clarity instead of confusion? If you need peace, direction, hope, and clarity for your future, then get ready. Don't allow yourself to get distracted or make excuses for why you can't finish reading this book. Everything will try to separate you from this message because it has the power to *change* everything! You cannot find purpose through knowledge alone; purpose is meant to be experienced!

Your purpose can be fuzzy because you simply haven't had enough life experience to make your direction clear. Life experiences help to shape your purpose. More importantly, it is experiencing God for yourself and gaining His perspective that allows everything in life to make sense.

It's in knowing Him that you become clearer on your purpose. This idea—experiencing purpose—is a concept we will unpack throughout this book. The original word for "know" in Biblical Hebrew is yada. It doesn't refer to intellectual knowledge; instead, it means to experience reality. In the Scriptures, "to know" means not just to be informed but to experience something. As Julia Blum says,

> *Knowledge is not the possession of information; it is an experience. To "know God" in the Bible is not "to know about Him" in some abstract and impersonal manner, not to grasp philosophically His eternal existence, but to recognize and experience His reality and to obey His will.*[2]

To know God is to experience Him. In the New Testament, Jesus says that, though many will say to Him, "Lord, Lord," He will tell some of them, "I never knew you; depart from me" (Matthew 7:21-23). To "know" means to have an intimate knowledge of the Lord. It isn't an intellectual knowledge. It's to experience Him as your reality. This is where you find purpose.

---

2 "SECOND Revelation: VA'ERA AGAIN," Biblical Hebrew and Holy Land Studies Blog - IIBS.com, 21 Jan. 2021, blog.israelbiblicalstudies.com/jewish-studies/second-revelation-vaera-again/?cid=32524&adgroupid=-1&utm_source=js-blog-posts&utm_medium=email_marketing&utm_campaign=bib_en_eml_js_posts_2016-07-14_32524.

Through experiencing Jesus and exploring the events and experiences in your life, we will show you how to accomplish the purpose for which you were created! You owe it to yourself to commit to this process and to make your number one project *discovering your purpose*!

Purpose is experiencing God's process of becoming all you were created to become so that you can intentionally accomplish all you were called to do for His glory. Why not you? Why not now—today? Let's get started.

CHAPTER 1

GOD'S PROPOSAL

Today was the day I was going to propose to my girlfriend! I remember waking up that day feeling both extreme excitement and extreme nervousness. My thoughts were consumed with joy and that "good kind" of anxiety. It was as if I were stepping into the biggest soccer game of my life.

My girlfriend and I had met two years prior, when I walked through the door of a youth ministry run by a friend of mine. I'd been trying to figure out what in the world to do with the teenagers I was now leading at my church. The person who greeted me was this short, cute Spanish girl named Karla. She smiled, looked at me, and said, "Hi. Who invited you here tonight?"

I said, "Pastor Steve did. I'm one of his friends."

Karla had this radiant smile that lit up a room, but I didn't think anything more of it than that at the time. Later, I would come to find out Pastor Steve was stepping down from his youth ministry, leaving a void in their church. Being that Karla was one of the main youth leaders, she asked me to come speak to their teens a few times until they found a new pastor. At the same time, she started to attend my youth group, just to hang out and hear me preach. This was the foundation of an amazing friendship that developed for a year and a half before we finally started dating.

About three months prior to the day I asked Karla to be my girlfriend, I had a dream that I was walking alone on a road, elevated high above wheat fields on both sides that stretched as far as the eye could see. Then, out of nowhere, I felt someone touch my hand. I looked over to my left and saw that it was Karla. She just smiled and didn't say a word. We walked off into the distance. I knew, at that moment, what this meant. In the Bible, wheat represents the harvest field, and God had called me to share the gospel around the world. I knew this meant that Karla was going to be by my side! I woke up that morning, looked in the bathroom mirror and said, "God, I know what you're up to, and I like it!" I knew I would marry Karla, who by that time had become my best friend. This was in January of 2003. Three months later, while lying on a blanket on Good Friday, I asked Karla to be my girlfriend. You could say that *was* a good Friday! Two months later, I bought a ring and held onto it until September 20th, when I would pop the big question.

Fast forward a number of months: Here I was, ready to propose to the woman I knew God had brought into my life. I took her horseback riding out by Disney. Ironically, she ended up having a blond-colored horse named Timmy! My horse was a brown one named Comma. Not quite Karla, but close enough. We laughed at the coincidence, made jokes, and had a blast together. It was like a scene out of a movie. Then, I took her to the amazing hotel at Universal Studios Portofino Bay to get her nails done! You know that scored some points. After that, we drove all the way to Ormond Beach, where everything was planned to come together. We stopped and had a romantic dinner at Carrabba's close to the beach, reminiscing about all our times together over the past few years. It was hard to eat because my stomach was in knots.

After dinner, I said, "Hey let's go to the beach and go for a walk, since we're close by." It didn't seem out of the ordinary, being that we both love the beach. Little did she know that my brother and sister-in-law, her best friend, and her best friend's husband, as well as the ones who introduced us, Pastor Steve and Sandra, would all be waiting behind the sand dunes at a special staged area. As we walked down the beach, I could see the space that had been set up—the red rose petals leading up to a blanket with a boom box on top. It felt like a million butterflies were flapping around inside of me. As we got closer, I said, "Hmmm. Would you look at that? Where in the world did this come from?"

I walked over and dusted off a hidden folding chair in the sand, and had her sit down. I pushed play on the boom box (this was before the days of iPods, Spotify, and smartphones). A song from the band Chicago called "Inspiration" began to play. I started singing the words to her: "You're the meaning in my life/ You're the inspiration." Both of us were teary-eyed. My heart was pounding.

After I sang the song, I got down on one knee and said something like this to her: "Karla, you are my best friend. I never knew God would have such an amazing woman for me. I've waited my whole life to find somebody like you. You're the most beautiful, kind, loving, and passionate woman I know. You're my best friend, my ministry partner, and I want to spend the rest of my life with you. I want to take care of you, protect you, provide for you, and make you laugh. I want to travel the world with you, have kids, and raise a family with you. I want to grow old with you and spend the rest of my life taking care of and loving you." Then, I pulled out the ring and asked her, "Karla, will you marry me?" She said yes, we both burst into tears, embraced, and kissed! Then, out of nowhere, our friends and family came running over the sand dunes screaming!

This was one of the most joyful and memorable days of my life. I made the best proposal I knew how to make. The only reason Karla said yes is because she had fallen in love with me, and I was offering to give her the life she'd dreamed of having. **No matter how amazing a proposal any man gives, it fails in comparison to what God has offered us.**

Now I know what you might be saying to yourself: *Here we go. He's about to push religion down my throat.* No—quite the contrary. I simply want to propose a scenario and share who the true Jesus of the Bible is, and His proposal to mankind. I'm only asking that you remain open to the possibility that there could be truth in what I am about to share. After you read through the rest of the book, you can decide for yourself. Just maybe your perspective on Christianity will change. It might just be that what you experienced growing up, witnessed at your parents' church, or heard in the media was, in actuality, a false gospel.

If you stay open-minded, you might just encounter the purpose of your existence. Either way, whether you are open to this viewpoint or not, if you follow and apply the principles throughout this book, I promise that they will change your life. You'll learn more about how you're wired and how to evaluate your life and make decisions for your future.

The proposal Jesus made to you and me is *good news*! He didn't just get down on one knee—He literally laid His whole life down on a cross and made the ultimate proposal anyone could make! He said in John 10:10 that He came to give us life, and life more abundantly. This abundant life is about living with a purpose! It is an amazing proposal.

Can you imagine a man making a proposal to a woman and saying things like, "I promise to never be there for you. I promise to cheat on you. I promise to never help with the dishes, clean the house, or help with the kids. I promise to spend all of our money, go into debt, and never share any of it with you. I don't want to take care of you, and I do not want to grow old with you. Our house will be full of stress and arguing, and I promise to make you miserable. I promise to never let you go out with your girlfriends, go out shopping, or get your hair and nails done"? No, that's crazy! What girl would ever say yes to that?

GOD'S PROPOSAL

God's proposal is the greatest one that has ever been given. It is the reason we live. To say "yes" to Him is to receive the greatest joy and fulfillment one can obtain. The proposal Jesus laid out to us can be trusted. He loves you. He created you on purpose, and He knows why you exist. Everything Jesus did and said was intentional.

If you wanted to fix something, how would you know the right way to go about it? You'd go to the owner's manual (well, nowadays, you can just YouTube it). If you want to fix your life, go to the Owner's manual: the Word of God. Just like biology is the foundation of being a doctor, the Bible is the foundation for finding purpose.

God's ultimate proposal is a life of purpose! The word "purpose" comes from a root word which means "to propose." The word "propose" means "to form or put forward a plan or intention, to make an offer or to set forth for acceptance or rejection."[3] We will either accept or reject God's proposal of purpose. To define your purpose means to discover the reason you exist, the intent for which you were created. Another way to say it is that purpose is a "means to an end." This carries the idea that objects are created and used to accomplish a specific purpose or task. They were not merely created for themselves.[4]

A cup is for holding liquid. A fork is for eating. A refrigerator is for keeping food cold. Scissors are for cutting things. A surfboard is for riding. A car for driving from one place to the next. These items do not exist by themselves and for themselves, but they exist to be used in a specific manner to make an impact. They were created to solve a problem. The most important thing is not that the cup just exists, but *why* the cup was created. Whom is it for? It is for the person who will fill it and use it to drink in order to sustain life.

In the same way, we exist and have been created by God to solve a problem—to carry out a task and perform a function. **God had a specific intention in mind when He created you. Problems reveal purpose!** The problem of Goliath revealed David's purpose. The Philistines were a huge problem to the Israelites, God's chosen people. David solved that problem by defeating Goliath and later became Israel's king. Just like David, we are the cup that God wants to fill with His Spirit so that we can be a source of life and blessing to others. We were not created for ourselves but to be a means to an end for someone else.

Everything Jesus did was intentional—every word He said, every person He talked to, every miracle He performed. Jesus never did anything without a purpose. We too must live our lives with purpose and intentionality if we want to maximize our potential. Psalms 139:13-14 says, "For you created my inmost being; you knit me together in my mother's womb. I praise you because I am fearfully and wonderfully made; your works are wonderful, I know that full well." You are not a mistake; you were handmade by God! You were knit together in your mother's womb and specially made for something great!

Jeremiah 29:11-13 agrees with this: "'For I know the plans I have for you,' declares the Lord, 'plans to prosper you and not to harm you, plans to give you hope and a

---

3 "Definition of Purpose." *Merriam-Webster*, *https://www.merriam-webster.com/dictionary/purpose*.

4 Andy Stanley. Podcast episodes: "September 2017: The Complexity of Purpose, Parts 1 and 2." *AndyStanley*, *https://andystanley.com/podcast/the-complexity-of-purpose-part-1/* and *https://andystanley.com/podcast/the-complexity-of-purpose-part-2/*.

future. Then you will call on me and come and pray to me, and I will listen to you. You will seek me and find me when you seek me with all your heart.'" Another version uses the words "hope and a purpose" in place of "future." God has specifically crafted you to do good works in order to bring Him glory. Ephesians 2:10 says, "For we are God's handiwork, created in Christ Jesus to do good works, which God prepared in advance for us to do." Another version uses the word "masterpiece." **You are not just a work of art; you are literally a masterpiece created by God Himself!** You are designed so uniquely that nobody else like you exists.

Walt Disney said, "Art was always a means to an end with me." Art is created not for itself, but as a means to an end—for others. Mickey Mouse wasn't created for himself; the fireworks that go off every night over the Magic Kingdom aren't for themselves. The rides the Imagineers created are not for themselves; all of these art forms are meant for guests and viewers to enjoy. They create magic and memories for families around the world. You are a work of art that was created not just for yourself, but to touch other people's lives! All these verses reflect the simple truth that you have been individually handcrafted for a purpose on this earth—to accomplish a task that only you can do.

You could have been born at any time in history, into any family, from any country. Why now? Why is your story the way it is? It is for a purpose. You were created for greatness, but it will only be found in being a means to an end. **Your life is meant to bring credit and glory to God and, in doing so, to lead others to Him.** This is the end goal. This book will unpack this purpose in the context of your specific life.

THE RIGHT QUESTION

I remember, from the time I was in high school all throughout my twenties, everyone asked me the same questions: "Tim, what do you want to do with your life? What do you want to be?" Maybe you've been asked these questions many times, as well. They're good questions. However, the better question is this: *What does God want you to do with your life?* During my younger years, many of life's most elusive questions arose. These are some of the ones you must wrestle with as you find your purpose, too:

- Who am I?
- What is the meaning of life—what's my purpose on this earth?

- How do I find my purpose, and how will I know when I've found it?
- How do I know if God is real? How do I know what He wants from me?

Proverbs 20:5 says, "The purposes of a person's heart are deep waters, but one who has insight draws them out." Your purpose is already in you! It's our desire that, as you read this book, the questions, stories, and principles within it drive you to probe and access the depths of your soul—to draw out what's inside of you. You were made for a purpose, and I want to help draw it out of you. Think of an old-fashioned well. You can't see the water from where you are, but if you turn the crank, lower the bucket, and lift it up, behold—there it is! In faith, you dive deep, knowing that something valuable lies down there. The questions and processes in this book are like that bucket, and your purposes are the water deep inside your soul.

THE PROBLEM IS REAL!

All this talk about purpose sounds great, but there's a problem: there is a battle going on for your life and purpose. Jesus tells us in John 10:10, "The thief comes to steal, kill and destroy, but I have come to give you life and life abundantly." The two scenarios facing us are destruction and abundant life! As a youth speaker, counselor, and coach, I have seen both. That's why I've dedicated my life to working with teens and young adults.

What causes destruction? In essence, a lack of biblical purpose. If you live *with* purpose, you'll avoid destruction and live the abundant life God offers. The enemy of your soul has a dark purpose: to bring destruction through a lack of biblical purpose. Every week, I hear heart-wrenching stories of brokenness and pain. Some of the biggest issues this generation is facing are depression, anxiety, insecurity, addictions, pornography, hopelessness, and suicide. According to Barna research, those aged 18-24 seek out porn at least once a month and are the largest demographic of internet porn consumers. They also report that 62 percent of teens and young adults have received a sexually explicit image, and 41 percent have sent one.[5] Further, Pew research reported that, in 2017, one in five teenage girls—nearly 2.4 million—had experienced at least one major depressive episode in the previous

---

5   David Kinnaman. "The Porn Phenomenon." Barna Group, published February 5, 2016. *https://www.barna. com/the-porn-phenomenon/.*

year. The total number of teenagers who experienced depression increased by 59 percent between 2007 and 2017.[6]

Dr. Jean Twenge, a professor of psychology at San Diego State University and author of *iGen*, says, "There is a mental health crisis among American teens and young adults." A recent study cited by *Time* reports that, between 2009 and 2017, rates of depression among those ages 14 to 17 increased by more than 60 percent. These increases were nearly as steep among those ages 12 to 13 (47 percent) and 18 to 21 (46 percent); rates roughly doubled among those ages 20 to 21. In 2017—the latest year for which federal data is available—more than one in eight Americans ages 12 to 25 experienced a major depressive episode.[7]

These stats are mind-blowing. The issues are real and complex. The attitudes I hear in regard to these issues are also alarming. This is part of why I wrote this book— to help combat these issues in our culture by offering truth, hope, and purpose to young people. While there are many factors causing destruction in our world, I believe one of the biggest ones affecting teens, young adults, and people in general is a life of *self*. **The biggest form of modern-day slavery is a life of self!**

Think about it: Most issues crippling our society can be traced back to people living for their own interests only. A life of self keeps one in bondage emotionally, mentally, financially, and spiritually. It's one of the biggest causes of pain in our world. Selfish choices and desires—greed—cause us to only look out for our own needs instead of looking out for those of others. Divorces happen, fathers walk away from families, people break the law, abuse occurs, people take advantage of others, and the lists goes on. A life of self causes people to become overwhelmed, stressed, depressed, unforgiving, and fearful.

The problem is not just purpose, but perspective. When life is all about you, you'll have no life. A life focused on self leads to destruction. A life of purpose will cause you to stop focusing on yourself and start focusing on others. When you stop believing your life is about you—that you're a means to your own end—you'll break free of the "selfie generation" mentality and the pressure to perform and

6   A. W. Geiger and Leslie Davis. "A growing number of American teenagers—particularly girls—are facing depression." *Pew Research Center, https://www.pewresearch.org/fact-tank/2019/07/12/a-growing-number-of-american-teenagers-particularly-girls-are-facing-depression/.*

7   Markham Heid. "Depression and Suicide Rates Are Rising Sharply in Young Americans, New Report Says. This May Be One Reason Why." *Time, https://time.com/collection/davos-2020-mental-health/5550803/depression-suicide-rates-youth/.*

please others. Until you do, life is reduced to what you want, how to please yourself, how to build your life around your best interests . . . and that way of living leads to destruction.

I believe this is why so many teens and young adults struggle with anxiety. According to the National Institutes of Health, nearly one out of every three adolescents between the ages of 13 and 18 will experience an anxiety disorder. These statistics, combined with the rate of hospital admissions for suicidal teenagers, also doubled over the past decade.[8] Chronic anxiety can lead to serious mental health problems: depression, substance use, and even suicide. Anxiety interferes with our ability to focus and learn, causing school problems that can have a lifelong impact. It can also lead to physical problems, such as headaches, chronic pain, digestive problems, and heart disease. Higher Education Research asks incoming college freshmen if they feel overwhelmed by all they have to do. In 2016, 41 percent of students said yes compared with 28 percent in 2000 and 18 percent in 1985.

Whether the culprit is social media, lack of sleep, increased scholastic pressure, screen time, broken homes, or any other number of factors, the verdict is simple: this generation needs help.

THE SOLUTION

For it is in giving that we receive.

—Saint Francis of Assisi

We make a living by what we get; we make a life by what we give.

—Winston Churchill

By now, you may be asking, "So what's the answer?" I'm glad you asked. The solution is God's proposal—living the purpose-filled, abundant life He promises in John 10:10. **The abundant life is obtained when you live out God's full purpose for your life.** One piece of that puzzle involves doing things not for self, but for others. This is a life of giving, not getting. Without this truth, life is unsatisfying.

---

8   Claire McCarthy, MD, FAAP. "Anxiety in Teens is Rising: What's Going On?" *Healthychildren,* *https://www.healthychildren.org/English/health-issues/conditions/emotional-problems/* *Pages/Anxiety-Disorders.aspx?utm_campaign=The%20Culture%20Translator&utm_* *source=hs_email&utm_medium=email&utm_content=80003220&_hsenc=p2ANqtz-_* *Q3yVWc74dQqmJMCPsma8erx7hOEwBB1DVU9mtCHae7txrMoLgvScktKlqhPcS_* *Yg0yyrXZOdabE8FFogFuuoJAGlVGg&_hsmi=80003220.*

God's purpose for you is that you live, in every area of your life, for the glory of God. He gets the credit for all we say and do. Colossians 3:17 says, "Whatever you do, whether in word or deed, do it all in the name of the Lord Jesus, giving thanks to God the Father through him." I love the part that says "in the name of Jesus," because this shows that you aren't taking the credit! When you do anything at all—cleaning, studying, working, or relating to others—do it unto the Lord. Jesus is our example of this selfless life: His purpose on earth was to give Himself for us. He said that He came not to be served but to serve (Matthew 20:28).

Scientific research proves that giving one's time, talents, and treasures is a powerful pathway to finding purpose, transcending difficulties, and discovering fulfillment and meaning in life. Allan Luks calls the euphoric feeling we experience when we help others the "helper's high." In fact, "In a study of alcoholics going through the Alcoholics Anonymous program, those who helped others were nearly twice as likely to stay sober a year later, and their levels of depression were lower, too.[9] Experts call this the "wounded healer" principle. Helping has a tremendous benefit for those receiving the help *and* for the helpers themselves.

Another researcher says that, through fMRI technology, we now know that giving activates the same parts of the brain that are stimulated by food, money, and sex![10] It has also been determined that "generous behavior reduces adolescent depression and suicide risk, and several studies have shown that teenagers who volunteer are less likely to fail a subject in school, get pregnant, or abuse substances."[11] The whole point is that God has hard-wired us to give. When we make things about others, it feels good! When we make life about us, we deprive ourselves of joy and meaning, even at a biological level.

Do you want to feel better? Do you want to reduce your levels of anxiety, depression, and addiction? Start living your life on purpose for a purpose. Live a life that gives to others. It will be the greatest high you've ever had! Giving is the cause of Christ.

---

9 Jenny Santi. "The Science Behind the Power of Giving (Op-Ed)." *Livescience*, https://www.livescience.com/52936-need-to-give-boosted-by-brain-science-and-evolution.html.

10 Jenny Santi. "The Secret to Happiness is Helping Others." *Time*, https://time.com/collection/guide-to-happiness/4070299/secret-to-happiness/.

11 Christine L. Carter Ph.D. "What We Get When We Give." *Psychologytoday*, https://www.psychologytoday.com/us/blog/raising-happiness/201002/what-we-get-when-we-give.

GOD'S GREATEST GIFT

The prerequisite for a proposal is intimacy. Nobody just asks someone to marry them without knowing the person. God's ultimate proposal is one of intimacy with Him. This is the essence of Christianity: It's about a trusting relationship with our Creator. It's exploring all the things that you can do, all the ways you can live, to experience peace and joy. Christianity isn't based on performance but on the grace of God. None of us are perfect—that's why we all need Jesus. He lived a perfect life and paid the price for all of our sins. But the only way we can live the way God has called us to live is from a place of intimacy with Him.

God's proposal is an abundant life. You and I have *one chance* to make this life count! He has called you to live out a radical purpose! It's about thriving, not just surviving. It's about waking up every day not dreading the day, but instead feeling that your life matters and you know what you want to do with it. Just like the blanket laid out in advance for my proposal, God has laid out a proposal for you and me that He prepared in advance. He is inviting you to step into your purpose— to say yes to His proposal—to live an abundant life full of His purpose, His joy, His peace, and His love. It is a life of forgiveness and second chances.

Living the abundant life is about living in His flow, not going against it. I remember one day, when my kids were little, we went to a water park in Orlando, Florida, called Wet 'N Wild. The park had a lazy river where you lie on tubes and float around in a giant circle, going with the current. My kids were in front of me and decided to ditch their tubes and swim in the opposite direction. After several seconds, they quickly realized this was an impossible feat. Getting scared, they began crying out to me for help. Living for yourself is like swimming against the flow of God—it creates fear and exhaustion. Living the abundant life, on the other hand, is about being fueled by God's strength and presence. When you have the presence of Jesus in your life, you have everything.

WHY THIS MATTERS

If you live for your own purpose and plan, you'll try to do it all in your own power, instead of living for God's purpose and plan and being fueled by His power. This is why so many people get burned out, fall into moral failure, or lose their joy, strength, and power. They're living out a self-made purpose; eventually, their power reserves run out. Choose to allow the presence of Jesus to touch your life today.

Even right now, just close your eyes and say, "Jesus, I want all that you've got for my life. I want your presence to be made real to me, right now. Consume me with your peace, power, and presence, in Jesus' name."

Your definition of success will determine your purpose. Is it money, fame, popularity, looks, things, influence? Or does it consist of relationships, health, fulfillment, joy, and quality of life? The *Oxford Dictionary* defines success as "the accomplishment of a desired aim or purpose."[12] You will hit the target at which you're aiming. I have defined that success for me is being faithful to what God has called me to do with my life, in how I live and treat others. When you take your last breath, what will be the most important things in your life? What will you be thinking about? You want to know that your life truly made a difference—that it counted for something and that you brought glory to God in what you accomplished!

This book will take you layer by layer through the difficult and abstract principles of accomplishing the task of hitting your life's bullseye. Each section will focus on a key principle that will be another brick upon the foundation of your purpose; over time, it will start to look like the house you are called to build.

I pray that this material puts you on a path of lifelong discovery of God's ultimate plan for your life. While it won't answer every question you have about your purpose, it will provide you with key principles to follow that will point you in the right direction. This is meant to be a concrete, practical guide to that path of purpose that can seem so elusive and abstract. May this book be a template that you can refer back to over and over again as you make decisions and listen to God's voice in your life. May the following pages awaken the purpose inside of you.

I had no idea what God truly had for my life. Had I known, I would have said yes a lot sooner. If He can take a kid who was broken, lost, with no way out, no purpose or direction, and suicidal, and use him to lead thousands of people to Christ all over the world, launching hundreds into their God-given purposes, then what can He do with *you*? It's time to start believing there's more to life than what you're experiencing. God is in the business of turning people's lives around, giving them new hope, a new meaning, a new purpose! I'm proof. It doesn't matter what sin you've been involved in—it's never too late to turn to Him.

---

12 "SUCCESS English Definition and Meaning." *Lexico Dictionaries | English*, Lexico Dictionaries, *www.lexico.com/en/definition/success*.

Purpose is experiencing God's process of becoming all you were created to become so that you can intentionally accomplish all you were called to do for His glory. Karla said yes to my proposal. How much more should we say yes to the proposal of our Creator? Will you trust God enough to surrender completely to the plans and purposes He has for you on this earth? In God's movie called Life, He is asking you to play your part, to live out the role He created specifically for you. If you say yes, you'll embark upon the most life-giving journey you can ever know. Today, Jesus is asking if you will trust Him. Will you take His hand and let Him lead you on this greatest of adventures? **Will you say yes to God's proposal?**

QUESTIONS FOR SELF-REFLECTION

How is the question, "What does God want you to do with your life?" different from the question, "What do you want to do with your life?" How does the first question cause us to change our perspective on what purpose truly is?

_____

_____

_____

Why do you think more young people are struggling with depression, anxiety, and other mental health issues today than ever before?

_____

_____

_____

Have you considered salvation as an intimate relationship between you and God? How does this change your perspective on what it means to say yes to Him?

_____

_____

_____

Is there anything holding you back from pursuing a (or deepening your) personal relationship with God? If so, what is it?

_____

_____

_____

CHAPTER 2

PILLARS OF PURPOSE

A year after the proposal came our big wedding day. I was standing at the altar after a full year of planning—this is the moment that can make any grown man weak-kneed, unglued like a teenage girl at a Justin Bieber concert. Karla's processional song began to play, and all eyes were staring at the back of the church. The double doors were flung wide open, and there she was: the most beautiful woman in the world, walking down the aisle. It was as if she were glowing with God's presence as she walked towards me. Our gazes locked. We were mesmerized, in the moment. My eyes filled with tears as I became overwhelmed with joy at the thought of becoming one with my bride.

As Karla got closer to me, the gazes of the guests shifted to me. If you've been to a wedding before, it's touching to watch the groom's face as he sees his bride come walking down the aisle. It brings a genuine feeling of love and joy to your soul. The ceremony was incredible. One pastor later said to me that, in the previous twenty years, he had not felt the love and presence of God at a wedding like he did that day.

God's proposal is about saying yes to the idea of living out our purpose—it's our yes to the truth that Jesus laid down His life for us. However, **marriage is the lifelong process and journey of obtaining the promises proposed.** It is the process of publicly living out that private decision to say yes to Jesus' proposal. Many excitedly say yes to the proposal, but then the marriage begins. Now, they have to live this thing out.

A strong marriage will take the tough seasons in life and use them to become stronger. Romans 8:28 (KJV) says, "All things work together for the good for those who love God and are called according to his purpose." I used to hate that term, "all things." *Really God?* I'd think. *All things? My parents' divorce, my soccer injury, working as a valet by Disney, the emotional and mental battles, the financial struggles?* The answer is yes. All things work for our good, but the key is the end of the verse: " . . . for those who love God and are called according to his purpose." If you love God and are committed to living out His purpose for your life, then you have the promise that He will use every situation you have ever faced for your good. If, however, neither of those things are true, the "all things" in our lives will never make sense or be used for our good. Many people decide to quit and never see God's promises come to pass. The decisions they make will divorce them from their destiny.

In this chapter, we're going to look at five key *Pillars of Purpose,* that will help define your purpose and help you apply the practical principles in the rest of this book. Let's dive in together and discover what's waiting for us in the covenant relationship that I pray you've said yes to already.

PILLAR #1: PURPOSE IS A PROCESS, NOT A ONE-TIME EVENT

Just like marriage, our purpose involves a lifelong process of discovery. I didn't just say, "I'm married now. I have arrived. There's nothing else to discover about my wife!" No! After fifteen years of marriage, two kids, running a ministry and traveling the world together, I am continually discovering new things about her. A marriage is a relationship with your best friend in which you do life together, make decisions, raise kids, chase after your dreams. Relationships are always changing. They're either growing or shrinking. When they become stale and stagnant is when they fall apart or die.

One central truth I've discovered is that purpose is a process, not a one-time event. Purposeful living entails constantly growing and changing. You will evolve and grow for the rest of your life. Here's a truth that reassures many young people I speak to: **You don't have to have everything figured out yet! It's *normal* to not know what's next.** Every season of life has a purpose, and your purpose isn't stagnant.

When I finally had my "Aha!" moment and said yes to becoming a youth pastor in 2001, after all those years of searching, I didn't throw my hands up and say "That's it. I've found my purpose. I'm going to be a youth pastor for the rest of my life." No way! That was the purpose God was calling me to *at that moment*. I had no idea it would grow and change as the years went on. I didn't know that, two years into being a pastor, I would start my own nonprofit organization called People of Purpose. I didn't know God would take me all over the world sharing the gospel. I didn't know I would use soccer and surfing as tools to connect with young people—that I would raise hundreds of thousands of dollars to fund all of these efforts—that God would take me all over the world to countries like El Salvador and Guatemala to do mission work. I didn't know I would travel to military bases in Europe and Asia, or places like Belgium, Germany, Italy, Japan, or South Korea—all for the purpose of reaching young people and sharing this very message with them. I didn't know I would be speaking to schools and church youth groups comprised of thousands of kids. I didn't know I would coach a high school soccer team that has become like my youth group and take them through leadership retreats, mission trips, purpose experience weekends, Bible studies, and group times. I didn't know that, fifteen years into my ministry, I would get my master's in pastoral counseling and begin to counsel kids professionally. Purpose is not stagnant. It continues to grow and build upon itself as you go through life.

Purpose is about the process, not the destination. Yes, we have a vision of accomplishing something—reaching our end goal. However, the destination, fun as it is, isn't the only thing we're after in life. If you miss the journey, you've missed the entire point. Part of why we're here is to enjoy the present path we're on while getting to our destination.

Since I live in Orlando, my family and I have annual passes to Disney. While we love going to the parks, half of the fun is the ride there. We turn on Disney songs, and each person gets to pick what song he or she wants to listen to next. Then, as a family, we sing loudly, laughing, giggling—especially when I start singing in a really high, intentionally-out-of-key voice, like a princess. As of late, we've been listening to the soundtrack of *Aladdin* with Will Smith as the genie. Even though our final destination is the Magic Kingdom, we always have just as much fun *driving* there as when we *are* there!

Many people think purpose is merely doing the things they feel called to do. For this reason, many are dissatisfied with life, even though they have so many blessings. There's always this underlying pressure to achieve more, be more, do more, because we think we haven't "arrived" yet and can't be happy until we do. Then, even once these people arrive at their destination and achieve their purpose, they *still* aren't happy. Why? Because the destination in itself was never the purpose. You have to enjoy the process! You may not like your current job; you may be frustrated at where you are in life, but don't lose hope! Your current situation is not your end destination. God has you where you are for a purpose. Learn what you can right now, trust Him for what's next, and enjoy the journey.

Hindsight is 20/20. Once you arrive at your career or destination, the process you experienced in getting there will make sense. This is what makes it hard for many to know what to do now, in the middle of the waiting and the confusion. What do you do? Focus on enjoying the journey. Live in the moment. That is the point—just like in the car ride to Disney with my kids.

Purpose is about taking intentional steps of faith, each day and in every season of life, that lead to a destination. The end result is that you live out your destiny, having lived a purposeful life. All the things I listed above were not in my five- and ten-year business plans. As I grew closer to Jesus, He began to unfold the next steps of my purpose. Things just fell into place. The process can be amended as needed, even when you make mistakes or veer off course. The process continues to expand. This is the lifelong journey God takes each of us through.

PILLAR #2: TWO MAIN PURPOSES

I believe we all have two main purposes in this life: a primary purpose and a practical purpose. Your primary purpose is permanent and never changes. It's spiritual in nature. Your practical purpose changes from season to season and involves what you're doing presently, day by day. Let's take a deeper look at both of these in turn.

Your primary purpose is your spiritual purpose on this earth. It is eternal. It's all about knowing Jesus and becoming who He has created you to be. Your primary purpose is about your relationship with Christ—being made into His image more and more each day.

God's eternal purpose is to reveal His wisdom to us through Jesus. Ephesians 3:10-11 (NKJV) says, "To the intent that now the manifold wisdom of God might be made known by the church to the principalities and powers in the heavenly places, according to the eternal purpose which He accomplished in Christ Jesus our Lord." God also confirmed the promises of His purpose for our lives through the oath made in the life of Jesus. Hebrews 6:17 says, "Because God wanted to make the unchanging nature of His purpose very clear to the heirs of what was promised, He confirmed it with an oath." An oath is a promise for all eternity. Romans 8:29 (author paraphrase) says, "God has predestined [His people] to be conformed to the image of his Son." Being made into the image of God means to be like Jesus. Since the beginning, God's primary and eternal purpose was for us to be made into the image of God—for us to become like Christ, heirs to His spiritual and eternal promises. Just like a child inherits all of his father's possessions, so too are we to inherit all the promises that are made possible through a relationship with Christ as revealed in Scripture. God's primary purpose for your life on this earth is eternal, permanent, unchanging!

This permanent purpose is an ongoing process. It never stops. In our past, our present, and our future, God is always at work making us into His image. Second Corinthians 3:18 says, "We all, who with unveiled faces reflect the Lord's glory, are being transformed into His image with ever-increasing glory, which comes from the Lord, who is the Spirit." Notice the phrase "being transformed" here. This means we are *continually* transformed into the image of Christ through the Holy Spirit. This is also a part of how "all things" in our lives are used to shape us into being more like Jesus. This is His ultimate spiritual purpose for our lives.

Your practical purpose, in contrast, is what you are doing *right now*, in this present season of life, to make an impact for God. This kind of purpose is temporary—it can change. Practical purpose involves being intentional with life and finding meaning in your current job, school, friends, or other circles of influence. If our faith doesn't affect our everyday living, it's meaningless. Purpose doesn't begin after you graduate, once you're married, or once you're in your dream career. Your purpose is where you are right now. It begins right at this moment. While you are waiting for God to move you into what's next, how are you living out your purpose in a practical way? How is God asking you to bring change for Him? What is He teaching you about yourself? How does He want you to grow? What does He want you to learn?

God has you in this present time for a reason. Make the most of it. **When you can embrace your present purpose, you will find joy in the journey.**

What's the purpose of God in your life right now, where you're at today? Don't overcomplicate it. Keep it simple. Too often, we put this huge pressure on ourselves of finding *the* gargantuan CALLING that we are meant for—a standard we constantly hold ourselves up against. Can I challenge you to replace that paradigm with a pursuit of your small, manageable, daily calling? Maybe your calling today is to go to school, work your job, and influence your friends, family or co-workers. Your present purpose prepares you for your future. God is at work, even if you can't see what He is doing. Trust the process!

PRIMARY PURPOSE	PRACTICAL PURPOSE
SPIRITUAL	NATURAL
PERMANENT/ ETERNAL/ UNCHANGING	PRESENT SEASON/ CAN CHANGE
BEING (WHO BECOMING)	DOING (RIGHT NOW)
RELATIONSHIP WITH CHRIST	RELATIONSHIP WITH OTHERS

PILLAR #3: LIVING A PURPOSEFUL LIFE IS MORE ABOUT BEING THAN DOING

Living with purpose is about being like the person of Jesus before doing the works of Jesus. What we do flows from our being (becoming) the people we are destined to become.

Soccer has always been a part of my life. I felt called to it as a part of my purpose at a young age. However, there came a point when soccer evolved from something centering around me to something that allowed me to coach and teach others. Prior to going into youth ministry, I found soccer a kind of "carrot" dangled in front of me—a guiding force that God used to lead me into a new purpose. At first, I couldn't figure out what He wanted me to do with soccer. What was the purpose behind it? Before He would reveal my next step, He had to internally transform me. As my heart changed—as I grew—my perspective on soccer shifted. I saw it as a means to an end instead of the end in itself. I saw it as a tool to fulfill my purpose of reaching young people. I realized that doing soccer ministry was secondary in priority behind becoming the man God wanted me to be.

Your primary purpose is about being; your practical purpose is about doing. Being comes before, and gives way to, doing. God is more concerned about you being molded into the image of Jesus than doing the works of Jesus. Philippians 2:13 says, "For it is God who works in you to will and act in order to fulfill his good purpose!" This says that He works *in* us first, so we can then *act* to fulfill His purpose. When you become more like Christ, you will do more of what He did on earth. **Doing is a manifestation of your character: who you are becoming.**

Part of your purpose is to become a disciple of Jesus Christ. Mark 3:14 (emphasis added) says, "He appointed twelve that they might *be with him* and that he might send them out to preach and have authority to drive out demons." Jesus' first calling, or purpose, for the disciples was to be with him. He wanted to so revolutionize the way they thought, talked, and lived. These men were called to be with Jesus for about three-and-a-half years before they were able to step fully into what they were commissioned to do! Then, in Acts 1, Jesus told them to wait in Jerusalem for the promised Holy Spirit. He said they would be filled with power: "Power to be my witnesses"! He didn't say to *do* witnessing first. Jesus knew the power of *being* would produce the ability to do all they were commissioned to do. Before the disciples ever went out and performed miracles, they learned to be with Jesus. This kind of purpose takes the pressure off; it's not performance-based Christianity. Yes, we are created to do good works, but that is because He first called us to *be* with Him.

God's will is not about a physical location so much as a spiritual condition. It's less about what you are doing and more about who you are becoming. In order for us to live out our biblical purposes on earth, our faith needs to become practical.

I've seen too many spiritually weird people whose faith never manifested in their everyday lives. **True biblical purpose means that our being must influence our doing.**

You may be thinking, *But I know a lot of people who are successful who don't follow Jesus.* Yes, this could be true; it is because those people are following the principles of Jesus, not the person of Jesus. They follow His principles of "doing" without even realizing it. They follow principles of goal-setting, commitment, having a vision, and building a team around them; however, they don't know Christ for themselves. That is how someone can become a multimillionaire, be at the top of his or her career, and still be miserable. Without the being, you merely have success that is void of purpose.

The world determines success based on money, possessions, influence, status, looks, popularity, or athletic ability. But the Bible looks at it through a completely different lens. Success is being obedient and faithful to the things God has placed you on this earth to do. God never called us to be *successful* in the worldly sense, but to be faithful. If we are faithful, success will follow automatically. True success is more about becoming who Jesus created us to be, having healthy relationships, and serving others.

PILLAR #4: YOUR PURPOSE IS NOT ABOUT YOU

My wife and I recently had lunch with a Disney Imagineer at Hollywood Studios in Orlando. Imagineers are the creative geniuses who make the Disney magic happen. I booked this luncheon because I was in the middle of writing this book and wanted some inspiration—I wanted to ask questions about the Disney truths and purposes that might coincide with what I was writing. As God would have it, we sat down with Brian Marschall, the lead designer at the Magic Kingdom.

During our three-hour conversation, I was dying to ask him a question about purpose. Towards the end of lunch, I finally had my window of opportunity. I said, "Brian, I have two questions for you. First, what do you feel is your main purpose working at Disney? And second, what is the purpose and goal of the art you create?"

His response took me aback. Almost without hesitation, Brian answered, "I'm a torch carrier! There is a very successful heritage and foundation laid by Walt himself." When he said that, my heart was racing! This incredibly creative and influential designer, without knowing it, was speaking about truths that parallel the spiritual principles of purpose. It's countercultural today—the idea that our purpose is not about us, but about those coming after us. Brian didn't say that he was trying to share his own message, make his own way, and carve out a name for himself. He was carrying the message of Walt and sharing *his* story.

His response to my second question added even more depth and context to this concept of purpose. He said, "The goal and purpose of my art is about creating a connection for a guest—to further the story, to enforce the story. If something stands out that's not truly part of the story, or the colors are off, people notice. If I do my job the right way, you'll believe that you are there, in that place, in the story. It's all about immersion and believability. It's the details that make that happen!"

Brian was saying that, while his life was about telling the greater story of Walt Disney, his art was the means by which he connected others to that story. If his art weren't consistent with the story, people wouldn't connect with or believe in it.

Your purpose is to be a part of God's story. Your life is the art and means by which others connect to and believe in His truth! If our lives aren't consistent with His story, we will fail to have a great impact on those we are called to influence. We are called to be torch carriers for Christ! Our lives are to be masterpieces that bring glory to God and His story.

I hate to break it to you but, contrary to what the world says, your life is not about bringing you glory, fame, material wealth, status, or followers. As Ephesians 2 makes clear, you were created to do good works in order to glorify God. Jesus says in Matthew 16:24, "If anyone would come after me, let him deny himself and take up his cross and follow me." We must deny the desires and cravings of the world that so many chase after. We must pick up our cross, our individual purpose on this earth, and follow the path Jesus laid out for us. To fail to deny yourself is to divorce from your destiny.

So many people are looking to find themselves, but they wonder why their dream life doesn't bring the fulfillment it seemed to promise. God didn't design us to live for ourselves. If you truly want to step into your purpose on earth you must first lose your life. Matthew 16:25-26 says, "For whoever wants to save their life will lose it, but whoever loses their life for me will find it. What good will it be for someone to gain the whole world, yet forfeit their soul?"

Purpose is that inner cry that wants to be a part of something bigger than ourselves. Having an eternal perspective takes your focus off yourself and puts it onto God. Life is short. We were wired for eternity. Ecclesiastes 3:11 says, "He has also set eternity in the human heart; yet no one can fathom what God has done from beginning to end."

C. S. Lewis said, "All that is not eternal is eternally useless." Your short-term purpose is a part of God's eternal plan. Second Corinthians 4:18 says we must "fix our eyes not on what is seen, but on what is unseen, since what is seen is temporary, but what is unseen is eternal." Only what we do that outlives us will matter. Our purpose is to live the life God created us for so that, at the end of this short journey, we have accomplished everything He put us on this earth to do. This is what leaves a legacy. This is the bigger story. It's all a part of His plan.

It's not our job to create our purpose. Instead, we willingly lay our lives down to God, and He reveals it to us! When we surrender and stop trying to figure it all out on our own, we'll discover a cause far greater than any we could have come up with for ourselves.

First Corinthians 6:19-20 says, "Do you not know that your bodies are temples of the Holy Spirit, who is in you, whom you have received from God? You are not your own; you were bought at a price. Therefore honor God with your bodies." When we make life about Christ instead of ourselves, we will be able to carry the torch of the gospel in a way that has an impact—we will fulfill the purpose for which we were created!

PILLAR #5: YOUR PURPOSE IS ONLY ACCOMPLISHED THROUGH GOD'S STRENGTH

Having had the privilege of counseling and mentoring hundreds of high schoolers, college kids, twenty-somethings, and adults, I have noticed a reoccurring theme: at some point in time, everyone has had life slap them in the face. They realize they don't have everything figured out.

It can happen at any stage in a person's life; it's inevitable. The typical scenario may look something like this: A teen discovers he doesn't know what to do with his future. A college kid is stressed out, he doesn't know what major to choose, he gets sucked into partying, and a girlfriend cheats on or breaks up with him. The college graduate finds that her job isn't what she thought it would be, or a married woman is left unfulfilled by her husband. Not living the Christian life and doing what he feels called to do merely leaves a man feeling overwhelmed and defeated. It is in these moments that we realize we cannot do things on our own. We were not created to carry the burdens of life and fulfill our purpose in our own strength. A few points on this follow:

1) *It is God's strength working in us that provides the ability to fulfill our purpose.* If it were obtainable in your own ability, it wouldn't be God. If you can fulfill your life's purpose without God, it's not big enough. Many times, we play it safe, settle for mediocre living, and dream small. We allow fear to get in the way, and so we live our entire lives never attempting anything significant for God. Only when we recognize God's role in making our purposes happen are we able to be who He called us to be and do what He has called us to do.

   Philippians 4:13 says, "I can do all things through him who gives me strength." The Greek used here is *endymamoō*, which means "to receive and increase in strength." It contains the root word *dunamis*, which comes from the same word from which we get the English *dynamite*. *Dunamis* means "to make strong and enable." It conveys the idea of an inward strength being provided. You cannot live this life on your own strength; trying will only lead to frustration. Look up. Stop trying to do it all on your own. Give God permission to step in and give you His strength.

2) *Fear paralyzes you and keeps you from pursuing your purpose.* The need to constantly be in control will keep you from tapping into God's strength. Most people never take action toward their dreams because they bow to fear, insecurity, and uncertainty.

3) *Fear puts confidence in your strength, while faith puts confidence in God's.* Fear isn't just the opposite of faith; it's a counterfeit. It causes you to put your belief in something other than God. It is an all-consuming, dominating, and

paralyzing emotion. Fear is about control. You know that fear is present in your life when you can't let go of control.

4) *Faith in God's power strips fear of its power!* When you place your faith in God's strength, fear is powerless. Understanding that our strength comes from Jesus is the key to overcoming fear. Fear says that our success comes from our own abilities; faith says that our success comes from God's abilities. While we will further address fear in a later chapter, it's important to know that you can only accomplish your purpose through God's strength when you surrender to Him. **Your level of strength is determined by your level of surrender.**

5) *Remaining in Christ is what brings God's strength.* In John 15:5, Jesus says, "I am the vine. You are the branches. If you remain in me and I in you, you will bear much fruit. Apart from me you can do nothing." Other versions use the phrase "abide in me." To abide means to *remain, dwell, continue,* and *stay connected to* Jesus. We are to stay connected to Christ if we want to manifest His fruit in our lives, which is the essence of purpose.

The fruit is not only our actions and habits but also the attitudes of our hearts, our thoughts, and our emotions. Our fruit is what others see. It's produced from the seeds we allow to be sown in our hearts. When we come to the realization that we truly can do nothing outside of being fully dependent upon God, we will remain in Him. He will give us the strength and confidence to move in faith and to live how we were designed to live. By staying connected to the source, we gain an unlimited supply of strength to accomplish the very purpose for which we were created.

QUESTIONS FOR SELF-REFLECTION

Why do you think we tend to see purpose as a one-time event, or destination, rather than a process? What cultural values influence this perspective?

_____

_____

_____

In your own words, explain the difference between your primary purpose and your practical purpose. Why is each one essential, and how do they work together?

_____

_____

_____

How does it make you feel to know that you don't need to create your own purpose, or find it all on your own?

_____

_____

_____

How does the idea of purpose being about Jesus (and not about you) make you feel? What do you need to change in light of this fact?

_____

_____

_____

Have you ever allowed fear to keep you from stepping into your purpose? If so, how? In what areas of your life do you need faith to become who God has called you to be?

_____

_____

_____

CHAPTER 3

THE PATH TO PURPOSE PART 1: IDENTITY

PART 1: IDENTITY

Upon graduating from college, I began living out my dream of playing professional soccer. This was before the MLS, or Major League Soccer, was formed—before you could make any actual money doing it, but at least I was able to travel and play in various cities and stadiums. I was on top of the world—so I thought.

One night, at practice, a guy tackled me and caused me to blow out my ankle. This was one month before I was supposed to go on a three-week mission trip to Bolivia with some soccer players. We were planning to play games against local teams and share the gospel. Because of my injury, I ended up not playing on the trip as much as I would have liked. But God was using this to teach me that soccer was not the most important thing. He had more for me. My heart was still hard at this point, and I was unwilling to listen to and obey what He was asking me to do.

My image had become wrapped up in being known as this likable, blond, blue-eyed surfing soccer player. However, upon returning from Bolivia, my professional playing days ended. I lost all motivation to train, quit playing mid-season, and spiraled into a year of increasing frustration. God was trying to get my attention—He was calling me to work with young people. This was information, but it had not yet become revelation to me, because my identity was in the wrong things. Until you start to align your identity with the right things, you won't find your purpose.

THE PATH TO
PURPOSE

| SALVATION > | IDENTITY > | AUTHORITY > | FREEDOM > | PURPOSE > |

There is a path that leads to purpose. When you understand this path, you'll see how these principles flow together and how you can allow God to build your life. **You can't step into your purpose unless you are living in freedom. You can't live in freedom unless you exercise your authority in Christ. You can't exercise your authority unless you know your identity in Christ. And you can't know your identity until you surrender your life completely to Christ and become His child!**

If you're living in sin and bondage, you won't have the ability to receive your purpose by faith. When I was frustrated, depressed, caught up in sexual addiction and shame, I did not have the faith or ability to believe the purpose to which God was calling me. I thought, *Who am I to think that I could help teens with their problems? Look at how I'm living right now!* However, when you experience the freedom Christ offers, it causes your faith to explode and your heart to open and long for His purpose! I'll spend the next few chapters building upon this concept of the path to purpose. These principles are simple—yet critical—to stepping into the life God created you to live.

WHO ARE YOU?

I want you to answer this question: *Who are you?* Take a second to think about it. Speak your answer to yourself out loud.

Let me guess: Your answer included some details about what you do, what you like, how you spend your days . . . right? That was me too. If you had asked me back in my mid-twenties, "Tim, who are you?" I would have said, "I'm a surfer. I'm a soccer player. I'm a Christian who loves his family and friends. I'm a valet. I'm an insurance salesman." I wouldn't have been able to go any deeper. These are things I did and liked, but they didn't define who I was. My identity and self-worth had come to be based upon my soccer performance—who I was on the soccer field. But who *was* I? I didn't know. This uncertainty left me at the mercy of others' opinions and the pressure to fit in with the crowd.

There is an identity crisis in America! It's an epidemic no different than what I went through individually. People don't know who they are. They take on any identity they feel suits them because they don't know who Christ is. How does this play out practically? We buy and wear brands with which we identify. Why? Because we aren't just buying clothes; we are buying an image. Think about your favorite brands of clothes, shoes, accessories, gaming systems, or cars. How does owning these brands make you feel about yourself?

My favorite brands of clothes are those related to surf culture: Hurley, Quicksilver, Billabong, and so on. I especially love wearing the Hurley label. Why? Because I identify with being a surfer. I believe surfing is about a lifestyle. It is cool, youthful, carefree, adventurous, adrenaline-seeking, and fashionable. When I wear those brands, I *feel* cool, hip, carefree, and adventurous! I feel good about myself—accepted—part of a unique subculture. The problem with basing your identity on the things you own is that it's a misrepresentation of what identity truly is.

WHAT IS IDENTITY, AND WHY DOES IT MATTER?

Identity is defined as "the distinguishing character or personality of an individual."[13] When people look at your life, what do they see? What words do they use to describe you? What are the discernible characteristics of your life and personality? Is what people see the real you, or do you try and project an image that's different from who you really are?

Taking on the right identity is key to living out your life's purpose. Identity is the most important topic in this current generation. When you don't know who you are, you begin to take on the identities of others. This keeps you from becoming the unique, authentic *you* that God created. You'll be hindered from discovering

---

13 "Definition of Identity." *Merriam Webster Dictionary*, https://www.merriam-webster.com/dictionary/identity.

your purpose until you know your identity. **God will not give your purpose to the person you** *pretend* **to be—He will only give it to the person He** *created* **you to be.**

Identity gives us the strength to be authentic, take off our masks, and be comfortable in who God made us to be. The higher our sense of identity, the more we realize who we are and whose we are. People who don't have a strong sense of identity lose themselves by living out others' expectations. *Peer pressure is only as strong as your identity is weak.* When your identity and worth are based on what Jesus says about you, others' opinions lose their power. Your self-worth is what helps you cope with life's adversities. It's what gives you the confidence to follow your purpose. Don't let your identity be a copy of someone else's! God has called you to stand out, to take off your mask and discover your true purpose. This chapter is meant to help you do just that!

There are two key parts of identity that we must discover in order to live out our purpose. **Just as there is permanent purpose and practical purpose, there is also spiritual identity and personal identity.** Both are equally important—they make up a two-sided coin. The spiritual side of your identity is who you are in Christ. The practical side is how you're wired: your personality, temperament, physical abilities, and so on. Both sides play an integral role in your purpose and how you view and adapt to issues in life. Let's look at each of them in turn.

PERSONAL IDENTITY

One of my mentors, Nelson Alsup, who has been a professional Christian counselor for over forty-seven years, says it is just as important to understand your personal identity as it is to grasp your spiritual identity. We will spend some time in later chapters unpacking this concept more, but in essence, here is what I mean: Your personal identity was created by God. He wired you a certain way. Understanding your passions, gifts, social style, and other aspects about yourself results in a certain confidence. Knowing your personal identity will help you in relationships, decisions, career paths, and every other area of life. For example, if you know that you're an introvert, you know that you'll probably be miserable in a sales job. If, on the other hand, you know that you're an extrovert, you'll probably anticipate feeling miserable in a cubicle where you don't get to talk to anyone all day.

If you haven't yet given your life to Christ, understanding your personal identity is an important step toward understanding your identity. When you begin to recognize and validate your gifts, it will open your heart to discovering the *giver* of those gifts, your Creator. If you're struggling in your faith, all I'm asking is for you to stay open to the possibility that there is a Creator, and that He made you just the way you are.

In the same way, if you are a follower of Christ, it's important that you discover your personal identity. Many love Jesus but have no idea what to do with their lives or how to discover what they are wired to do. They don't know their personal identity and, therefore, don't make much of an impact. Understanding your personal identity can take you from a place of surviving to a place of thriving!

Research shows the importance of finding your personal identity. One in three college students changes his or her major, and one in ten changes it twice or more times.[14] The U.S. Bureau of Labor Statistics says that today's young adults will have 8 to 10 jobs by the time they are thirty-eight.[15] A thirty-seven-year-old study was released in 2019 which showed that individuals held an average of 12.3 jobs from ages 18 to 52, with nearly half of these jobs being held before age twenty-five. Men held 5.9 jobs from ages 18 to 24, compared with 1.9 jobs from ages 45 to 52. Of the jobs that workers began when they were 18 to 24 years of age, 70 percent ended in less than a year, and 93 percent ended in fewer than five years. Among jobs started by 35 to 44 year olds, 36 percent ended in less than a year, and 75 percent ended in fewer than five years. [16]

These statistics reveal a few important things. First, our world is rapidly changing. Second, most people don't know their personal identity and what their purpose is—they're simply jumping from job to job. Third, even if you do know your personal identity, your purpose is truly a process that unfolds over time. The older you get and the more jobs you hold, the clearer your purpose becomes. You realize where your gifts and passions lie more and more as time goes on.

14 "Beginning College Students Who Change Their Majors Within 3 Years of Enrollment." *Data Point: U.S. Department of Education*, https://nces.ed.gov/pubs2018/2018434.pdf.

15 "The next era of human-machine partnerships: emerging technologies' impact on society & work in 2030." *Institute for the Future and Dell Technologies*, https://www.delltechnologies.com/content/dam/delltechnologies/ assets/perspectives/2030/pdf/SR1940_IFTFforDellTechnologies_Human-Machine_070517_readerhigh-res.pdf.

16 "Number of Jobs, Labor Market Experience, and Earnings Growth: Results from a National Longitudinal Survey." *Bureau of Labor Statistics: U.S. Department of Labor*, https://www.bls.gov/news.release/pdf/nlsoy.pdf.

There is also often a disconnect between what you learn in college and what you do in the workforce. In 2013, a Federal Reserve researcher found that 27 percent of college graduates were working in a job that matched their college major; 38 percent were in jobs that did not require a college degree at all.[17] On one hand, we could argue that these percentages could change if more graduates discovered their personal identities earlier. However, on the other hand, this research confirms that finding one's personal purpose is a process that we all undergo. Just as jobs are developing every day, so too are you becoming something you were not yesterday. Your personal identity will change—and that's a good thing!

Eighty-five percent of the jobs that today's students will do in 2030 don't exist yet, the Institute for the Future has predicted. How do you prepare for a future and job market that is unknown? By discovering your personal and spiritual identity! This is a key piece of discovering purpose.

Each of us needs to find our own path. College isn't for everyone. Growing and continually being educated is. The bottom line is this: understanding your personal identity can save you money on a college education you didn't need or classes you didn't have to take. It will help you capitalize on future job opportunities as well as eliminate unfitting career decisions in your early years. It can even save you from marrying the wrong person! All of these benefits are priceless.

Discovering your personal identity and utilizing your skills in a practical way will be covered in depth in the second half of the book. Personal identity is critical in fulfilling your purpose; however, it is only one piece of the puzzle.

SPIRITUAL IDENTITY

Knowing your personal identity isn't enough. Why? Because it has limitations. Most people become frustrated when they find their personal identity and experience superficial success, but still feel lost and purposeless. Deep down, they know they were meant for more, but they can't figure out what that more is. They don't know where they fit into the kingdom of God—they don't know their spiritual identity.

---

17 Gretchen Frazee. "How colleges are preparing students for jobs that don't exist yet." *PBS*, https://www.pbs.org/newshour/economy/making-sense/how-colleges-are-preparing-students-for-jobs-that-dont-exist-yet.

Personal identity leads to success, while spiritual identity leads to significance. No matter what stage of life you're in, you may have achieved some success; you *don't* necessarily have significance. There's a difference! Success garners wealth, status, influence, and accomplishments. Significance is achieved when you use your influence to make an eternal impact on someone else's life. Therefore, true fulfillment only comes from knowing how your personal identity fits into God's overall plan to build His kingdom on earth. Unless you come to embrace this truth, you will be left feeling empty.

In our culture, we have different forms of identification. There are drivers' licenses, school IDs, work IDs, birth certificates, and passports. These give us special rights and privileges—access to things we otherwise wouldn't enjoy. I travel a lot, and every time I go into a new country or re-enter the United States, the authorities ask to see my U.S. passport. Without my passport, I'd never be able to access other countries. It serves as verification of my identity. In fact, I had to submit my birth certificate to even apply for a passport! It's just another layer of proving who I am—my identity.

Just as my passport and birth certificate verify my identity, being born again through a relationship with Jesus guarantees my citizenship in heaven as a child of God. Because we are children of God, we have an inheritance—the right access to every spiritual blessing and promise He has given us. In order to step into our purpose, we must first believe what He says about us and our identity!

Personal identity alone won't help you live out your true purpose. Identity is more than your race, culture, gender, clothing, possessions, relationships, physical prowess, or skills and abilities. All of these will leave you empty if they aren't laid upon the foundation of your true, secure identity in Christ.

Identity is the foundation of purpose. If Satan can steal your identity, he can steal your purpose. This is why your spiritual identity is so essential—because the identity that comes from being in Christ, being citizens of heaven, can *never* be stolen. It has the greatest anti-theft protection ever. Galatians 2:20 says, "I have been crucified with Christ and I no longer live, but Christ lives in me. The life I now live in the body, I live by faith in the Son of God, who loved me and gave himself for me." Colossians 3:3 echoes this assurance: "For you died, and your life is now hidden with Christ."

At the core of identity is the idea that when we give our lives to Jesus, we become brand new people. We become spiritually reborn, a new creation. Second Corinthians 5:17 (AMP) says, "Therefore if anyone is in Christ [that is, grafted in, joined to him by faith in him as Savior], he *is* a new creature [reborn and renewed by the Holy Spirit]; the old things [the previous moral and spiritual condition] have passed away. Behold, new things have come [because spiritual awakening brings a new life]." This means that all of our old identity, our past sins, our old ways of thinking and living, are now dead, and we have been resurrected to a new identity and life in Christ with a new purpose.

Our identity is to be in Christ first; then everything else falls underneath that. **God does not ask you to deny your race, culture, or background, but to recognize that those things come after your kingdom identity.** Any self-sufficiency outside of a life fully surrendered to Christ is a false identity. Having our spiritual identity intact is what gives us access to lives of true, eternal purpose.

MADE IN GOD'S IMAGE

Your spiritual identity is who you are in Christ. Who does Jesus say you are? Genesis 1:26 (KJV) gives us insight: "And God said, 'Let us make man in our *image*, after our likeness.'" We were made in God's image! The words "image" and "likeness" convey the idea that we are representative figures—models—of God. We are reflections of our Heavenly Father, in the same way children are reflections of their biological parents. When you align with your spiritual identity, it creates a settling in your soul because you are aligned with the purposes of God. Any other identity is a false identity!

Genesis 1:27 restates verse 26 but adds another part: It says, "So God created man in His own image, in the image of God he created him; male and female." This is God's intended purpose for humankind—being created in His image. When we get this foundational truth wrong, it creates all kinds of dysfunction. Identity is deeper than skin color, nationality, skills, or passions. At its core, identity begins with being a child of God. My son and daughter have some amazing qualities: they're smart, athletic, funny, caring, compassionate, and artistic—just to name a few. They also each have areas that need work. I don't love them based on their performance. I love them simply because they're my kids. This is the kind of love upon which identity is built.

ADOPTED AS HIS CHILDREN

When we give our lives to Jesus, we are adopted into the family of God. Our salvation and status as His child isn't earned by performance—going to church or doing all the right things. It's simply given to us through faith. First John 3:1 says, "See what great love the Father has lavished on us, that we should be called children of God!" Likewise, Romans 8:15 says, "The Spirit you received does not make you slaves, so that you live in fear again; rather, the Spirit you received brought about your adoption to sonship. And by him we cry, 'Abba, Father.'" The Greek word for "adoption to sonship" is a term referring to the full legal standing of an adopted male heir in Roman culture. Being that this passage was written in a time in which the Jewish nation was under Roman rule and domination, people understood what the apostle Paul was trying to say (Romans 8:14-16).

It is confidence in our identity that gives us the ability to live out God's destiny. We don't do things in an attempt to *gain* an identity, but because we've *already been given* our identity. Understanding who we are strips away the pressure of performance. This empowers us to live out our purpose from a place of acceptance. When we operate out of our God-given identity, we align ourselves with heaven's resources—joy, peace, hope, strength, faith, maturity, finances . . . the list goes on. We trust that God will take care of us, open the right doors, and provide all that we need. Because we are God's adopted children, we can have confidence in who we are instead of living in fear!

KARLA'S STORY: THE GIRL IN THE RED DRESS

A few years back, my wife Karla and I received some life-changing news. Her former stepfather, Richie, called me one morning and said, "Tim, I need to share something with you. Karla is adopted. Miriam is not her biological mother."

I was sitting in a Bank of America parking lot at the time; I could barely comprehend what I was hearing. "What? Karla is adopted?" I asked. "You've got to be kidding me!" The weight of this news was like a bowling ball in my stomach. I went to her mother's house immediately and confirmed that it was true. Karla's family had kept this secret for over thirty years!

As it turns out, Karla was born in El Salvador. She had grown up living there with her grandparents and in California with her mother, Miriam. Karla's grandfather owned a trucking company in El Salvador, but during times of violence and political upheaval, Miriam left the country and went to California with Karla.

The story of how Miriam had come to care for Karla was the part we hadn't known before. The truth was that Miriam had been unable to physically have kids of her own, but she wanted a little girl. A friend of Miriam's had a co-worker with a live-in maid at that time (a common practice for upper-middle class families in Latin America). This young maid was in her twenties and had just given birth to her third child—a girl. The maid's mother didn't even know she had this new baby yet and would never have let her keep the baby, so the maid was willing to give her up for adoption—to Miriam. When Karla was three months old, Miriam went over to her friend's house. The maid walked down the hallway carrying a beautiful little girl in a red dress. Miriam took Karla into her arms and brought her home. Karla's life and destiny had been forever altered in that moment!

Regardless of whether or not you agree with Miriam not telling Karla about her adoption, she decided so because she didn't want her to feel she wasn't special—second rate. Her adoption was an amazing act of love. Who knows how different Karla's life would have been had Miriam not made the decision to adopt her? Karla thought she was born into a wealthy family in El Salvador, with a grandfather who owned a trucking company. Her feeling of worth and value could have been tied to where she came from, her looks, her talents, or her popularity. However, she now had the opportunity to live out what she'd been teaching all of her years as a Christian.

She understood that her worth was not from superficial, earthly things, but that her identity truly did come from being a child of God. Karla learned these principles when she gave her life to Christ at thirteen years old in a small private Christian school in San Salvador, El Salvador, called Josue Iglesia Christiana. These foundational truths now gave adult Karla the ability to absorb and receive the newfound discovery of her adoption. In fact, this revelation gave her an entirely new appreciation for how we have been adopted by God!

SPIRITUAL IDENTITY COMES FROM KNOWING OUR HEAVENLY FATHER

There are certain parts of your identity you inherit from your father. In most cases, you get your last name from him. Some children grow up without a dad, and so take on their mother's last name. Either way, the point is that your parents provide you with identity. In the same way, **we get our true spiritual identity from our Heavenly Father.**

As a pastor and counselor, I've found that many people who never knew their fathers have something in common: they grew up with deep feelings of rejection, believing that they weren't good enough. Those are lies. Ephesians 1:4-5 (author's paraphrase) says, "Even before the world, God loved us and chose us in Christ to be holy and without fault in his eyes. God decided in advance to adopt us into His own family by bringing us to Himself through Jesus Christ." When we choose to give our lives to Jesus, we are adopted as His children and given all the rights and privileges that entails. You go from lost to found, from rejected to accepted, from failure to freedom, from fatherless to fathered, from alone to alongside Him! This is what empowers us to overcome rejection and fear.

Even though Karla never met her biological father, she knew that her identity was in her Heavenly Father. This spiritual identity is what has given her stability, peace, and confidence her entire life. She's traveled the world, speaking to thousands of young people, visiting orphanages, churches, schools, and military teen camps to share about finding identity and purpose through Christ! Who would've thought that this baby girl, born to a poor maid, could be called to such a purpose? It all began with the foundation of identity—what she believed about herself.

OUR POSITION: SAINT OR SINNER?

Identity is not about performance; it's about position. Many people profess to be sinners saved by grace. If you've given your life to Christ, that is who you *used* to be—but that is not who you are now. Positionally, you are now a *saint* who sometimes sins. That's how God sees you.

Satan can't take away your saint status. He wants to deceive you into believing lies about who you are in order to keep you living the lowest level of Christianity he can. Most of the time, this looks like believers trying to perform better—to be better. The Christian life, however, is not a matter of trying harder; it's a matter of trusting more!

The Bible refers to us as "saints" or "holy ones" around two hundred times, and to unbelievers as sinners around three hundred times.[18] We have been changed from those unholy and sinful to those who are called saints. Isn't that amazing? God calls you and me "holy ones!" We changed from people who could not help but be displeasing to God—objects of wrath—to people who share the nature of God Himself (2 Peter 1:4)!

You may be thinking, *Well, Tim, I don't feel very holy right now.* That's the point! This is why so many people stay stuck in sin and bondage for decades. You have to change the way you believe and the way you look at yourself. As believers, we're not trying to *become* saints, we *are* saints who are becoming like Christ. God has given us a new position. In Ephesians, the phrase "in Christ" is used around forty times. Clearly, it must be important. Second Corinthians 5:17 says that if anyone is in Christ, he [or she] is a new creation. The old is passed away and all things are made new. This means you are a new person—whether you feel like it or not. It's important that you start believing this about yourself. As one study guide puts it so well, "God doesn't fix your past—He gives you a brand new nature. He makes you a new creation. He sets you free from your past."[19]

So many in our culture believe lies about themselves—that they are somehow less than others (or more, which can be equally as devastating). If you believe you are inferior or useless, you'll behave that way. If you believe that you're dirty or abandoned, you will act that way. If you believe that you're trash or rejected, then you will behave like trash. **Right believing leads to right behaving. You're not saved by how you behave but by how you believe!** Romans 10:9 (ESV) says, "If you confess with your mouth that Jesus is Lord and believe in your heart that God raised him from the dead, you will be saved." It doesn't say "Those that behave properly shall be saved." Your behavior will follow your beliefs! When you believe the right things about your life, your behavior will follow those beliefs.

DEBI "ARIEL" AND ELISHA "SPIDER-MAN"

When my daughter turned three years old, we had a Little Mermaid birthday party. One of her presents was the Ariel princess dress. She looked so cute wearing it! A few months later, when my son turned five, he got a Spider-Man mask. When

---

18   Cindy Bergenback. "We Are Saints Who Sin." *FICM*, https://ficm.org/neilsblogs/we-are-saints-who-sin/.

19   Neil T. Anderson. *Freedom in Christ Small-Group Bible Study Student Guide.* Gospel Light, 2008. 6.

Debi put on her dress, she would walk around the house singing the song from the movie that Ariel sings. I would start to join her, but she'd quickly tell me, "Daddy, stop singing! Only *me* sing."

When Elisha put on his mask, he became Spider-Man. He ran around the house pretending to shoot webs at me, and telling me that I couldn't move. He jumped off couches and bolted around the house, making all the appropriate sound effects. "I'm Spider-Man!" he'd say.

Everything inside of my children believed they were Ariel and Spider-Man. As soon as they put on the clothes, they became the characters. When you take on the character and identity of a child of God, it will cause you to think, act, and talk differently. It will allow you to see yourself the way *God* sees you! This is the beginning of stepping into your purpose.

The bottom line is that we need to change how we think about ourselves. If you think of yourself as a sinner who is lucky enough to know Jesus, you'll likely keep on sinning. If, however, you see yourself as a saint—a child of God, worthy of being loved, saved, and given new hope—then you'll start living differently. Don't get me wrong; being a saint doesn't guarantee that your behavior will be perfect. First John 1:8 says, "If we claim to be without sin, we deceive ourselves and the truth is not in us." The difference is that saints are no longer *controlled* by our sinful natures. We have the ability to obey God—a choice we were previously powerless to make—because of the Spirit of God in us. What you believe about yourself will lead to your ultimate spiritual purpose: being made into the image of Christ.

IDENTITY LEADS TO AUTHORITY

Your identity gives you the ability to exercise your authority and obtain all that God promises you. I remember when my son was about four years old. Before bed one Friday night, he asked me for lemonade in a sippy cup. I told him, "Son, we don't have any, but Daddy promises he'll get you some lemonade tomorrow."

Elisha knew that, when Daddy made a promise, he always followed through. Well, let's just say I didn't expect him to take me up on my promise as quickly as he did. That next morning, at about seven a.m., he came walking into my bedroom and tapped me on the arm. "Daddy, wake up. I want lemonade."

I remember barely opening my eyes. "What?"

"Daddy, I want lemonade."

"I know Buddy. Just go back to bed, and I'll get you some lemonade later."

Elisha started smacking me on the shoulder, hard. "Daddy wake up! You promised me *lemonade!*"

I tried to stay asleep, ignoring him, hoping he would go away. His little bony fingers began to pry open my eyelids. "Son, Daddy is really tired. Let me sleep, and I'll go to the store later."

He repeated, "Daddy, you *promised* me lemonade."

At this point, I knew I'd better follow through—he wasn't going to leave me alone until I did. So I got up, threw on a hat, and jumped in the car to go to Walmart. I bought Elisha's lemonade, came home, filled his sippy cup with it, and put him back into bed. He looked up at me, completely content, a big smile on his face. Daddy made him a promise, and he knew he could politely but boldly demand that I follow through with it.

Let me ask you this: how many people do you think have the audacity to come into my bedroom while my wife and I are asleep—to walk in without knocking—and wake us up? Nobody other than my children would do that. I'm close with my brother and sister, but even they wouldn't do that. They don't have the authority or the right to access my private chambers without my permission. I didn't have to verbally tell Elisha this. He just knew that, as my son, he had the authority to access Daddy anytime he wanted.

Just recently, I reminded Elisha of this story. I asked, "Why in the world did you think it's all right for you come into my room and wake me up like that?"

With a big smile and a giggle, he responded, "Because I'm your son."

Our identity is about who we are—our position as God's kids. We have full access to him through what Jesus did for us! Our identity carries authority. **Authority** provides access. **As a child of God, you have every right to access the throne room of God.** He has made us promises in this life, and we have the authority to come to Him when we have a need. We can approach Him and say, "Daddy, you promised us peace. You said that I don't have to be anxious—that I can bring my requests to you. You promised freedom—that I am more than a conqueror, that I don't have to live in fear. God, you promised me an abundant life—a life of purpose! I am going to keep coming to you and asking you for it because you are a good God and you always fulfill your promises."

We must come boldly to our Heavenly Father and access every right, privilege, and promise He has set forth in Scripture. Until we truly gain understanding of our identity, we will not believe we are worthy of having—let alone living out—a purpose!

AUTHORITY

Jesus says in Ephesians 2:6 that we are seated with Christ in heavenly realms. Being seated with Christ indicates that we share in His authority. My son's identity gave him the authority to access me privately; on the other side of the coin, I *gave* him that privilege and that freedom.

This is, oftentimes, where the younger generations get in trouble and end up living in bondage. Many in this generation want to be free—to call their own shots and meet their own needs instead of seeking God to meet their needs. Being able to do what you want isn't freedom. That's called anarchy! Chaos. It only leads to self-indulgence and bondage. We want to be our own authority, but God didn't design us that way. He designed us to be under authority—for our protection, freedom, and ultimate good.

There is a difference between power and authority. **Power is the huge semi-truck going down the highway. Authority is the small motorcycle cop on the side of the road who, simply by pointing his finger, can pull over that giant truck.** The reason the cop has that authority is because he has been given it by a higher power: the government. In the same way, we have been given authority as children of God. Jesus said in Matthew 28:18 that all authority in heaven and on earth had been given to Him. Then, in Luke 10:19, He said that He has given believers all authority to overcome the power of the enemy. If we are going to walk in freedom, we must understand how to exercise our authority!

When my daughter was six years old, somebody broke into our house during the daytime, while we were gone. They smashed in my bedroom window and ransacked the room. They stole my family heirloom World War II handgun, passed down from my grandfather to my Uncle Al—a Vietnam vet—to me. They also stole all of my wife's jewelry. For a few months after this attack, my daughter and son were afraid. At bedtime, they would ask me, "Daddy, are the bad guys going to come back again?"

I prayed with them each night and helped them learn how to take authority over their own thoughts and emotions. They would repeat after me a prayer like this: "Jesus, I take authority over this fear that's trying to keep me scared. I command the fear to leave me. Fear has no authority over my mind, my emotions, or my sleep. Jesus, I know you are protecting me, so I ask you to give me your peace instead of fear. Thank you for loving me and putting your angels outside of my bedroom and around our house. In Jesus' name, Amen." It took a few weeks, but the fear completely left both of them, and it did not have control over their lives.

James 4:7 (ESV) says, "Submit yourselves therefore to God. Resist the devil, and he will flee from you." The word "submit" here means to come under the authority of something. The reason so many Christians are getting beat up spiritually is because they are not coming underneath the authority of God and His Word! When we're under His authority, we have the authority to point our finger and command the devil to flee.

If we don't exercise our authority as children of God, the enemy will continue to steal our peace, joy, and purpose. The starting point to spiritual victory is coming before your Heavenly Father and allowing Him to reveal your identity and His love for you. This love is the foundation for your spiritual identity, and it brings stability to your life. It gives you the ability to feel safe so that you can fulfill everything you were created to do. It leads to freedom. Freedom is the next requirement to discovering and living out your purpose in such a way that you impact the world. In the next chapter, we're going to explore freedom and why it's so important.

QUESTIONS FOR SELF-REFLECTION

Before reading this chapter, how would you have answered the question, "Who are you?" How would your answer to this question be different after reading this chapter?

_____

_____

_____

Why do we absolutely need to know our identity if we want to step into our purpose? How does NOT knowing our identity hinder us from fulfilling that purpose?

_____

_____

_____

In your own words, explain the connection between knowing your identity in Christ and wielding spiritual authority.

_____

_____

_____

_____

Why is identity about position and not performance? How does this change your perspective on your own identity?

_____

_____

_____

_____

In what ways do you need to wield your spiritual authority more? Spend some time in prayer and in the Word, seeking God's help in this area.

_____

_____

_____

_____

CHAPTER 4

THE PATH TO PURPOSE PART 2: FREEDOM

PART 2: FREEDOM

When I think back to my twenties, I'm extremely grateful for the freedom I now have in my life. There were periods when I was so confused, frustrated, stuck, and afraid that it felt like I would never find my purpose. The gospel I'd heard my whole life—the idea that God had a plan for me—seemed out of my reach.

At other times in my younger years, I thought I was *living the life*. Surfing, soccer, sex. I mean, what better life could there be for a guy in his twenties? But when the temporary happiness was gone, something deep in me cried out for more. I wasn't living in freedom; I was bound in sin. When those cycles of sin came and weighed me down, they caused discouragement, doubt, fear, and confusion. No matter how hard I tried on my own, I could not break out of these habits. **Though I loved Jesus, I was living for myself, trying to figure out my future *my way*.**

It wasn't until I realized some simple truths that I was able to step into the life I now live. The principles of freedom turned my life around—and they can do the same for you. God set me free from sexual sins, suicidal thoughts, anger—from feeling lost, stuck and purposeless. Becoming free requires you to take an honest look inside yourself and see the areas that keep you in bondage. If you embrace these truths, you'll be able to unlock the same freedom in your life and begin stepping into the reason you exist. If you are ready for a fresh start, read on.

BELIEF AND FREEDOM

Our first home was a townhouse located on a pond. One day, while I was praying, I kept hearing this loud yelping, screaming noise. I got up and went to the window, but didn't see anything. Returning to pray, I heard the sound again—even louder! I ran back to the window, thinking, *What in the world is this?* This time, I looked into our neighbor's fenced-in yard and spotted some type of small animal attacking their dog. Naturally, I did what any guy would do: I grabbed my video camera. I filmed for about a minute, just to see what would happen, before doing the next logical thing—at least in my mind. I called 911! Can you imagine being on the other line of this call?

"911, what's your emergency?"

"Um, yes. There's some kind of small animal attacking my neighbor's dog. It looks like a badger . . . I can't tell, though."

"Excuse me, sir? Are you saying there's a badger attacking a dog in your neighborhood?"

"Yes. The dog can't get away, because she's on a leash chained to a stake. Can you please send an officer out here? I'll be outside." I hung up, put on my soccer shoes in case this savage thing came at me, and I had to kick it, and ran over to my neighbor's yard with no shirt on, carrying a big stick.

"Hey!" I yelled. "Get out of here!" The creature took off and dove back into the pond. I began calling to the dog to try to get her to calm down, because she was still yelping and running back and forth. I could see that her face was bloody and mangled from the bites. I thought about jumping the fence, but quickly remembered that a wounded animal I didn't know could be dangerous. I didn't realize until the officer arrived and we watched my video together that the animal guilty of this attack was a sea otter!

The police were able to track down my neighbor, the dog's owner. When he came home, I showed him the video. The yelps were so high-pitched and loud that it's almost unbearable to listen to (you can see the actual video footage of this encounter in the video series that goes with the workbook). The neighbor's response will forever be etched into my mind. As soon as he saw, it he said, "That demon otter! If only she hadn't been chained to the leash, she could have jumped up onto the dock and defended herself!"

I asked, "What's your dog's name?"

"Angel!"

When he said her name, it hit me. His dog's name was Angel, and he'd referred to her attacker as "that demon otter." I started considering the implications of this scenario. The Lord used it to show me a metaphor: the battle for freedom between angels and demons in the spiritual realm. The spiritual realm is extremely real. We are in a battle. Angel was a black lab-pit bull mix—a tough animal. However, because she was tied to the stake, she couldn't fight as she was designed to do. She was like today's generation—chained up. The otter, like the culture, continues to attack. On the outside, these cultural attacks may look cute and harmless—we may think that messing with sin is no big deal. In the end, however, those who aren't prepared get attacked and end up crying out for help—answers, freedom, meaning, and purpose.

We need to get to higher ground. What's this higher ground? It's like the dog being able to get onto the dock, the higher ground, so she could have been protected and fight from a higher position. It's understanding and believing the truth about who you were created to be. This is why we spent the previous chapter focusing on identity. **True identity gives us the ability to exercise our authority. We're not fighting for victory, but instead enforcing our authority in the world through the truth of the Word of God.** This is the fight of freedom, and living a life of freedom is what enables you to step into your purpose.

PURPOSE PREVENTERS

Remember that our road map and path to purpose begin with surrendering to Christ. When we do this, we find our identity, which allows us to exercise our authority. Finally, this results in living in freedom and stepping into our purpose. Many ask if being free is important to fulfill their purpose. Yes! Even if you figure out what you want to do with your life, you will eventually be exposed, crash and burn, have a moral failure, fall into an addiction, or life will just crush you. We can't allow anything to prevent us from walking in the freedom to which Christ has called us.

Just like the chain prevented the dog's freedom, there are many issues in culture that keep people in bondage. **I describe bondage as anything in your life that has become bigger than God—both the "good" and the "bad."** Bondage causes us to tolerate and trade dysfunction for the truth that leads to freedom. Purpose preventers, then, are those things we tolerate and trade for the truth.

I have the privilege of speaking to, counseling, and praying with thousands of teens and young adults every year. The recurring general issues that keep these young people in bondage are widespread. Many are dealing with fear, depression, anxiety or stress, addiction, worry about the future, finances, health issues, family issues, and so on. I believe there are two main lies in today's generation that keep people in bondage and prevent their purpose.

The first lie is, "I can be my own God." This is a lie of autonomy for those who want to live independently of God. They believe that they can figure things out on their own, and that they don't need God or anyone else to tell them how they should live. Essentially, it's a form of self-worship.

Worship means showing reverence and adoration for something—normally, a deity. It originally comes from two words, *weorth* and *ship*. "Weorth" means "worth." "Ship" is an old English word that means something of shape or quality. It's also where we get the words "friendship" and "sportsmanship." Worship, then, is showing value, or worth, to something. When we worship God, we declare that He is worthy and has value! We completely give ourselves to God, spirit, soul, and body, because of who He is and what He has done. Worship is surrendering our will for His purposes, so that our lives can truly reflect His glory to others.

This comes down to control. Those who don't worship God want to control their own lives. They don't trust God's plans. Proverbs 3:5-6 says, "Trust in the Lord with all your heart and lean not on your own understanding. In all your ways acknowledge him and he will make your paths straight." Trusting in self and controlling our own lives will lead to bondage—even if it doesn't seem like it at first.

The second lie is, "I am not good enough." Everything in culture reinforces this message. Social media causes us to play comparison games and shouts that our life isn't as good as somebody else's. We aren't as good-looking, athletic, or smart as he is. We don't have as much money as she does. We don't get to travel like his family does. We don't have as many friends or followers as she does. We begin to determine our self-worth based on likes, views, and follows. A generation that's become focused on self is now suffering with more anxiety and lack of peace than any other. Much of it comes from the lie that we are not good enough.

Whatever you follow is what you'll emulate. Whatever you emulate, you will value and worship. Whatever you worship, you will serve—it will become your master! We say we want to be our own person, live our own life—be free. But then we live just like everybody else. That's not freedom; that's called following, and it's one of the biggest forms of bondage in this generation.

Both of these lies are rooted in pride! Pride is what caused Lucifer to be kicked out of heaven. Pride has two sides to it. It's not just thinking too highly of yourself (Lie #1), but it's also thinking too little of yourself (Lie #2). **Biblically speaking, pride is any view or opinion of yourself that's contrary to God's view—how He made you.**

What other lies are prevalent in our culture? Say a few out loud to yourself, or write them down. What are the lies you've believed about yourself? Maybe they include the following:

- It's not cool to be a follower of Christ.
- Jesus is a fairy tale.
- Partying will make my problems go away.
- If I could just have a good-looking guy/girl by my side, I'd feel valuable.
- I can listen to or watch whatever music, shows, movies, or photos I want, because they don't affect me.
- If I just make a lot of money, or have nice things, I'll be happy.

One of the biggest and most specific lies in today's culture is that pornography is no big deal—that you can look at it without being affected by it. "There aren't any long-term consequences," this lie says. "You can stop any time you want." Or even this one: "I'll quit when I get married." Let me tell you something from behind a counselor's closed doors: These are *all* lies! If you're dealing with this issue, you'd better address it now, or it will destroy your future (or current) marriage!

Research says that pornography has reached epidemic proportions. According to the Conquer Series, 66 percent of high school boys look at porn once a week.[20] Other articles state:

- 62 percent of teens and young adults have received a sexually explicit image, and 41 percent have sent one (usually from/to their boyfriend/girlfriend or friend).[21]
- 57 percent of young adults ages 18 to 24 report seeking out porn at least once or twice a month.[22]
- 70 percent of men and 30 percent of women watch porn every week.[23]
- *90 percent of teens and 96 percent of young adults* are either encouraging, accepting, or neutral when they talk about porn with their friends.[24]
- Porn sites receive more regular traffic than Netflix, Amazon, and Twitter combined *each month*.
- 88 percent of scenes in porn films contain acts of physical aggression, and 49 percent of these scenes contain verbal aggression.
- It's projected that virtual reality (VR) porn should be a $1 billion business by the year 2025. That's in third place, behind an expected $1.4 billion virtual reality video game market and a $1.23 billion VR NFL-related market.[25]

According to my experience, I personally believe these statistics are low. I can tell you this: Most high schoolers are actively looking at porn 2-4 times a week. It's become so ingrained in culture that it's now widely accepted. One of the indicators

20 "The Conquer Series." *Kingdom Works Studios.* Updated 2020. https://conquerseries.com/.

21 David Kinnaman. "The Porn Phenomenon." *Barna Group*, https://www.barna.com/the-porn-phenomenon/.

22 "Teens & Young Adults Use Porn More Than Anyone Else." *Barna*, https://www.barna.com/research/teens-young-adults-use-porn-more-than-anyone-else/.

23 Alexis Kleinman. "Porn Sites Get More Visitors Each Month Than Netflix, Amazon and Twitter Combined." *Huffpost*, https://www.huffpost.com/entry/internet-porn-stats_n_3187682.

24 "Pornography Statistics." *Covenanteyes,* https://www.covenanteyes.com/pornstats/#stats_title.

25 Ibid.

of this issue is indicated by the fact that only one in ten teens and one in twenty young adults say that their friends believe viewing porn is wrong.[26] Statistics will change over the years, so I don't want to focus too much on them other than to demonstrate that this topic is one of the greatest battles of our generation. This epidemic is a full-out attack against this generation, against healthy relationships and marriages, and against how God created us. Pornography will distract you from your purpose! It's a counterfeit to real intimacy—the kind that only comes through Christ. Pornography will fill you with fear and shame. It will isolate you and pull you into captivity. It has the potential to disrupt and invade your future life, your marriage, and your self-worth. This issue must be resolved if you want to live out your purpose.

What's holding you back from stepping into a life of freedom? What areas of your life continue to grip you, chain you down, tempt you? What are those cycles of sin—the habits that you just can't seem to break? Fear? Anxiety? Depression? Pride? Pornography? Shame? Doubt? Maybe something happened in your past that was painful. Maybe it's unforgiveness toward someone who wronged you, and you can't seem to let that go. It could even be the loss of a loved one that you blame God for—that you can't seem to move past.

You don't have to be a slave anymore! You can get to higher ground. Jesus *is* that higher ground! He wants to set you free. There is hope for every area of bondage in which you find yourself. There's a deeper level of freedom available to you. Once you experience the freedom of Christ, you will *never* be the same!

FREEDOM

> *Once a man has tasted freedom he will never be content to be a slave.*
> —Walt Disney

So what *is* freedom? Where does it start, and how do we get it? Freedom is a continual state of surrendering control of every area of your life to Christ and being filled with His Spirit to live the life for which you were created. More simply put, **freedom is living life as a child of God who is totally surrendered to the Savior.**

---

26 "Porn in the Digital Age: New Research Reveals 10 Trends." *Barna Group*, https://www.barna.com/research/porn-in-the-digital-age-new-research-reveals-10-trends/.

There's a flow to walking in freedom. So many times, we focus on the problems in culture, which I refer to as symptoms. Walking in freedom requires looking deeper than the surface and getting to the root cause of bondage.

I remember a bush in my front yard that had burrs on the branches. I'd cut it down, and months later, it would grow back. I poured bleach and other chemicals on the stump, but it always grew back! This went on for a few years, until I got tired of it, bought a shovel, and dug it out. The roots were bigger and deeper than I expected—no wonder it kept growing back! Treating the symptoms only is like trimming a branch from the stump—it's only a temporary solution.

How do we get to the root cause of our bondage and dig it up? How do we walk in freedom? Transformation begins in our thoughts. If you want to experience God's emotions, you have to take on God's thoughts and beliefs. Everyone wants peace, joy, and fulfillment. These are characteristics of Christ. In order to change the ways we feel, we must change the ways we think. Romans 12:2 says, "Do not conform to the pattern of this world, but be transformed by the renewing of your mind." Transformation begins in the mind—with our thoughts and beliefs. The word "conform" has two parts: "con" and "formed." What is a con artist? Someone who lies and deceives. This verse is saying, "Don't be fooled or formed by the lies of this world."

Freedom begins when we expose the lies we've believed and replace them with the truth. If you want to live out your purpose in freedom, it begins with examining and refining your beliefs. According to Christian psychologist Dr. Neil Anderson, behind every bondage in your life is a lie you are believing. For example, the lies I believed in my twenties included the following:

"My mom rejected and walked out on me."

"God is at fault for my parents' divorce."

"I am valuable based on my soccer accolades, my good looks, and the attention I get from girls."

All of these were lies. I allowed the enemy to deceive me. In fact, my mom and I had a great relationship throughout the divorce, and we've always been close. This just goes to show how Satan attempts to twist the truth and affect our beliefs and, ultimately, our freedom.

The power behind deception is that, by definition, you *don't even know you are being deceived*. We focus on the lie instead of the truth. It was deception that caused the first sin back in the Garden of Eden. Satan convinced Adam and Eve to do things their way instead of trusting in God. Today, we're no different. We want blessings in the natural, but continue to live lives of sin and rebellion against God. We've taken matters into our own hands, and we've attempted to be our own gods! You have power over what you believe, but what you believe has power over you! Your behavior will follow your beliefs.

What was God's antidote to this pride and rebellion? He sent Jesus into the world to provide healing and forgiveness—physically, mentally, emotionally, and spiritually. The freedom we are looking for has already been accomplished in the person of Jesus. The question is, will we run to Him and trust Him to be our source of freedom?

Whatever you run to in your time of need is your savior! All of us are prone to self-medicate by turning to things other than Jesus to cope with life. We look for relief, but it's temporary. Whatever you put your hope into, if that thing exits or leaves your life, then you are left hopeless. Running to these things *instead of* Jesus keeps us in slavery. There's nothing wrong with stress-relieving activities, but approach God first. Running to friends isn't bad, unless it replaces running to Jesus. Remember, there is a practical component to freedom and a spiritual component. I love to surf and play soccer to relieve stress, but these things cannot replace God. Surfing instead of going to God would be sinful. Combining the two is the best. In fact, some of my *best* prayer times have happened when I'm out in the ocean.

At this point, you may be wondering, *Why does any of this matter? Do I really have to address the messed-up areas of my life?* Yes! Don't fool yourself. I've watched many young people grow up and never face their issues. The results are devastating. Unless you get to the root of what's holding you back and find true freedom, you'll remain a slave to sin and self. This slavery will prevent you from living out your purpose. As my friend Pastor Jeff Krall says, "Slaves don't build their dreams!" You can't live out your eternal purpose as a slave.

THE SOLUTION

What holds you back from pursuing God's purpose and feeling qualified to step into the life He has for you? What sins or issues are holding you back? What is the tug-of-war inside your head? For me, it was anger, lust, rejection, and fear. I was afraid that God would ask me to give up these things in order to say yes to His plan. I wanted control. I believed the lie that my plans and ways were better and more enjoyable than what God would call me to do. I was deceived.

As we've said, deception has always been the strategy of Satan; therefore, *truth* is the beginning of freedom. **To step into freedom, we must become brutally honest with ourselves and with God.** Until we get honest—until we know the truth—we'll remain deceived and in bondage. Herein lies part of the problem. What *is* truth? Today's generation doesn't believe in absolute truth. Instead, many believe that truth is relative. However, believing something doesn't make it true automatically. You can believe all day that, if you jump in front of a moving train, it won't hit you; that doesn't change the truth that you will be squashed as soon as you decide to jump.

In John 14:6, Jesus says, "I am the way, the truth and the life. No man comes to the Father but by me." Jesus didn't say He *has* truth, or is *a piece of* the truth. Jesus said, "I am *the* truth!" Jesus is the one who sets the captives free. There is no truth outside of Christ and His Word. Therefore, according to Dr. Neil Anderson, the power for the believer comes in knowing and choosing the truth.[27]

How do we break free of bondage? True freedom requires having a truth encounter. We can't do this until we know the truth. John 8:32 says, ". . . [K]now the truth and the truth will set you free." It's not the knowledge itself that frees us, but the subject of that knowledge. The contextual audience of this verse was Jews who *knew about* God in their heads, but didn't *know* the person of Jesus! The phrase "set free" used here carries the picture of being liberated morally. Just like physical death liberates us from debt, so too when we intimately know Jesus and surrender to him, we are liberated from any bondage to sin. Knowing Jesus, the Word of Truth, eliminates the power of sin over our lives.

The ultimate change involves confronting the lies we believe by bringing the Word of God into our situation. John 1 says that Jesus is the Word. When we bring the Word into our situation, we are releasing the very Source and Person of *freedom*

---

27   Neil Anderson. *The Bondage Breaker.* Harvest House Publishers, 2019. 24.

into our lives! Galatians 5:1 says, "It is for freedom that Christ has set us free." Jesus doesn't just have truth. He *is* truth. When you invite Jesus into your situation, you're inviting Truth and Freedom Himself!

True freedom comes as we expose the lies we believe and replace them with the truth. When I was younger, one of the lies I believed was that I needed to find my value in girls and sex. It was based on my need to feel like a man by being accepted and validated by women. I never could put my finger on the reason why. Clarity didn't come until years later, when I recognized that, at some point in time, I'd felt rejected and abandoned by my mom because she divorced my dad and moved out. I felt like she'd left me, too. Even though we had a great relationship after the divorce, I allowed the devil to deceive me. Things began to change as I allowed God to expose this lie and replace it with the truth of His Word. I never felt that insecurity again. It seems so simple now, but it took me years to figure out.

HOW DOES JESUS SET US FREE?

Freedom comes from the blood of Jesus. Colossians 1:14 (KJV) says, speaking of Christ, "In whom we have redemption through his blood, the forgiveness of sins, according to the riches of his grace." It is the blood of Jesus that cleanses us and sets us free from the power of sin and death.

How can we be sure that Jesus has the power to set us free? Because Jesus is eternal and omnipresent, He is in our past, our present, and our future. If Jesus can forgive you of your sins from the past, that means He can go back in the past and bring healing to all wounds and brokenness. He can heal all of your pain and sorrow. He can free you from shame or unforgiveness.

John 8:36 says, "So if the Son sets you free, you will be free indeed." We must recognize that the only source of true freedom is Christ! The word "indeed" means, "really, truly, and unquestionably." Jesus made these statements to Jews who claimed to be Abraham's descendants and, therefore, to never have been in bondage to anyone or anything. Jesus was changing and challenging their thinking when He told them that whoever commits a sin is a slave to sin. He wanted them to understand that everyone has sinned. **Every single person needs Jesus to set them free as only He can!**

The word picture I like to use when I explain this freedom concept is that of someone standing in front of a judge, waiting for his or her verdict. They've committed a crime, but the judge decides to acquit them. In a courtroom, the judge would say, "This case is dismissed." He'd slam his gavel down, and that would be the end of it. God is the holy and righteous Judge. When we ask Jesus to forgive our sins, He comes in and cleanses us—He frees us from our past. He takes His holy gavel and slams it down with authority, declaring that we are free to go. Nobody can reopen our case again. We cannot be retried for our crimes. Our case has been dismissed and closed forever!

CONVICTION VS. CONDEMNATION

Sometimes, the hardest part of becoming free is forgiving *ourselves*. We beat ourselves up over and over again. In essence, we're trying to reopen our case, even when we don't realize it. This is where condemnation comes in. It's different from conviction. Many confuse the two in the same way they confuse guilt and shame.

Conviction is from God, and takes place when God brings to our attention a sin in our lives. Conviction is an inner feeling that what we have done is wrong. Conviction comes from the two biblical words for "convict" and "convinced." It therefore means, "to be convinced of sin" or "to have a convinced conscience." The word convicted is only used once in the Bible—in John 8:9 when a group of men brought a woman accused of adultery to Jesus. Jesus challenges them, causing them to leave one by one. The Scripture says they were "convicted in their conscience." Jesus then asked the woman, "Where are you accusers?" and said, "Neither do I condemn you. Go and sin no more!" The accusers felt conviction because they became convinced of their own sin.

Guilt is another way to describe conviction. Guilt is the human emotion felt in response to the spiritual principle of conviction. When we do something wrong, we feel guilty. We have a choice to respond to this feeling in a way that leads to freedom. Disregarding the prompting of the Holy Spirit, on the other hand, can lead to bondage.

Condemnation is distinct from conviction because it's from Satan. Shame is the human emotion brought about by spiritual condemnation. Romans 8:1 says, "Therefore, there is now no condemnation for those who are in Christ Jesus." Shame and condemnation are *not* from God. They are designed to beat us up over and over again—to destroy us.

Shame is what the men who brought that woman to Jesus were trying to inflict upon her. Often, it's what the enemy uses against us when we sin, as well.

Guilt says, "I did something wrong." Shame says, "There is something wrong with me." **The byproduct of guilt and conviction is hope. However, the byproduct of shame and condemnation is hopelessness.** One produces hope and repentance while the other produces hopelessness and despair.

How do we recognize the difference? You can recognize condemnation and shame when you've asked Jesus to forgive you, but you still feel like beating yourself up over your sin. Often, this results in us asking God for forgiveness over and over and over again. Our thoughts bombard us: *I can't believe I did that again! Look what you did! You call yourself a Christian?* The end result is that we feel trapped and condemned. That's condemnation. That's shame. Recognize it, and don't receive it!

The blood of Jesus brings freedom by empowering us to embrace conviction and by exposing condemnation for the lie that it is. When we bring our thoughts, actions, and emotions to Jesus and confess our sins, He is faithful to forgive us. This is why we stated in the last chapter that your identity is so critical to your purpose. When you understand you are a child of God, it removes all shame. Forgive *yourself*, therefore, in agreement with His forgiveness. Walk in freedom and move on!

Freedom is not the absence of sin but the presence of the Savior! Second Corinthians 3:17 says, "Where the Spirit of the Lord is there is freedom!" Are there any areas in which you're not walking in freedom? Have you denied the Spirit of the Lord access to any areas of your life? When you allow His presence in, it will bring true freedom. Any area of your life where there is bondage is an area in which you haven't fully allowed the Spirit of the Lord to have control. We have to bring the secret things into the light!

"DADDY, BLOW ON IT!"

One time, when Debi was young, she fell and skinned her knee. She was bleeding, and didn't want me to touch it—let alone put hydrogen peroxide on it. She said, "Daddy, don't touch it. It hurts. That medicine is going to burn!"

I said, "I know, honey. But that's how it will heal. If you don't let Daddy touch it, I can't clean it."

After putting the peroxide on, the stinging set in. Debi said, "Daddy, please blow on it." As I did, the burning sensation decreased and eventually went away.

What an illustration for many of us! We say, "No, Jesus—don't touch *that* area of my life. It's too painful. You can work in any area but that one." However, when we allow Jesus to pour the truth of His Word over our lives and blow upon our hearts, His healing power flows and brings freedom.

A similar story took place when Elisha was about eighteen months old. He had a fever for about five days that would spike as high as 106 degrees. He had a rash from head to toe and felt miserable. I took Elisha to the doctor, and they discovered he had a rare sickness called scarlet fever. The staff had me hold him down while they checked him, which included putting a rectal thermometer somewhere Elisha did *not* appreciate. He was screaming and staring at me as if to say, "Daddy, why are you letting them do this to me?" Heartbroken, I held him against my chest, watching him scream and squirm as the doctor inspected him.

After five days of this and no change in his condition, I was exhausted. I felt helpless. Then, something happened that is forever seared into my mind. Elisha had just woken up from a late afternoon nap; he came walking down the hall towards me. He was shirtless, diaper sagging, looking miserable with his bright red rash. Elisha put his hands up in the air and locked eyes with me, crying, "Dada!" When he got to me, I picked him up and held him tight, rocking him side to side. His diaper rested on my forearm, its contents squeezing out through the sides and onto me. In that moment, I began to cry and pray over him with passion, saying, "In the name of Jesus, I command this sickness to leave my son's body. I declare that healing will flow through his body and this fever will break. I declare that Elisha will be made whole." As I prayed this over him, Elisha went limp in my arms, and became totally at peace. You could feel the presence of God in that hallway. Instantly, his fever began to lower. By the next morning, it was gone. The bright red rash had totally disappeared!

Many of us may have bondage, sickness, darkness, or parts of our lives that need freedom and healing. Notice that when Elisha came to me, I didn't say, "Get away from me, you disgusting sick little midget. Go get healed, and then I'll hold you!" No! I said, "Come here, son. Come to me as you are—dirty diaper, rash, tears, confusion and all. Just come to me." So many times, we think we have to clean ourselves up before we come to God. God is saying, "Come to me as you are. I can handle it all. I'm not grossed out by your junk. I just want to hold you and set you free!" Will you bring your dirtiest junk, your biggest bondage, your darkest secrets to Him today? Will you let God heal you?

The path to purpose is through the doorway of freedom. **Finding freedom isn't about performance; it's about surrendering to the truth of your identity in Christ.** It's about letting go of your way and trusting in His way. When you embrace your identity in Christ, exercise your authority as a child of God, and walk in freedom, you will be on the path of purpose.

QUESTIONS FOR SELF-REFLECTION

What "purpose preventers" can you identify currently in your own life that are holding you back from your purpose? How is each of these things a hindrance?

_____

_____

_____

Which of the two lies in this chapter do you tend to believe more: "I can be my own God," or "I am not good enough"? Why do you think that is?

_____

_____

_____

Do you tend to feel convicted or condemned when you sin? How can you tell the difference?

_____

_____

_____

What stood out to you about Tim's stories of his children at the end of this chapter? Does this shed new light on the nature of your relationship with God?

_____

_____

_____

CHAPTER 5

POSSESSED WITH PURPOSE

"Modern religion focuses on filling churches with people;
the true gospel emphasizes filling people with God."

—A. W. Tozer

As you read this chapter, my prayer is that your heart is stirred like never before—stirred to believe for the impossible in your life! I pray that the presence of Jesus will literally invade your soul as you read these words. Stop and pray right now, at the start: "Lord, have your way in my life. Speak to me, and open my heart to receive your presence in a profound way. Holy Spirit, flood this very room right now. I want to encounter you!"

CHRISTIAN'S STORY

I'll never forget one night of youth service in Deland, Florida. I'd just begun a new youth pastorate position, and I didn't know the youth there yet. God singled out one of the young men and gave me an impression about his life. What occurred that night has altered the course of this young man's, Christian's, life.

Christian recounted the following:

> *The night I really met the person of Jesus was Tim's second week as our youth pastor. I was thirteen or fourteen. The room was full with teens. In the middle of his sermon, Tim stopped and asked me to stand up. He proceeded to say things to me that there's no way he'd know unless God showed him. Tim told me that God wasn't mad at me—that I didn't have to hold on to guilt and shame. He specifically said something about walking in victory. This was only the second time Tim had met me. He had no idea that, just a few weeks before, I'd told my parents I was struggling with pornography. I'd thought I was unlovable. I know we read stories about God's love, but it wasn't until the moment I heard a stranger tell me the exact thoughts in my own mind that I knew God's love was true. At that moment, it wasn't Tim speaking to me. It was Jesus. It was a turning point in my life. If I hadn't let go of the guilt and shame and walked in victory, I never would've been able to live out my purpose.*

Soon after this encounter, Christian began leading worship and went on a mission trip to El Salvador. After he graduated, he did a year-long internship with my ministry, People of Purpose, in which he led worship at youth camps, conferences, churches, schools, and U.S. military bases! He went all over the world—to El Salvador, Belgium, South Korea, and Okinawa—living out his dream and purpose as an eighteen year old. Shortly thereafter, Christian went to Southeastern University in Lakeland, Florida, where he became a part of the highly sought-after worship team, SEU Worship! He now has a full-time position leading worship and working with youth and young adults.

Christian reflects, "I thought I was unusable. God used me. I thought I was disqualified for ministry. God qualified me and opened every door I've walked through. The moment I found purpose changed my life. It wasn't the moment I planned out my whole life—I didn't. It was the moment I met the person of Jesus!"

The night that the presence of Jesus consumed Christian ensured that he would never be the same. It started him down a path of pursuing the presence of Jesus and, consequently, living out his purpose—even though he didn't see the plan ahead of time.

Jesus doesn't set you free just so you can sit around with a smile on your face. He wants to give you a new nature, a new identity, and He wants to possess you with His purpose! When His purpose consumes you, there is no force in hell that can stop you!

WHAT ABOUT ME?

Are you someone who thinks this is true for others but not for you? Maybe you've heard the sermons and attended church for years, but you still have a hard time believing it could happen to you. Our current circumstances can make us feel as if God loves others more than He loves us—that we are, somehow, flawed believers. Many times, people are left wondering, *Why does God speak to them but not to me? Why did God give them a breakthrough but not me?*

If you're feeling this way, you may need to experience—either for the first time or in a fresh way—the power and presence of Jesus! You aren't a flawed believer; there just may be something holding you back. You may need to come under the anointing that breaks off that bondage. It could be as simple as getting on your face alone before Jesus and encountering Him; it could be praying with someone who has the faith you are lacking at this moment, so that Christ's grace and love can wrap around your life and do something that you can't do on your own. You need to encounter the power and presence of Jesus!

JESUS WANTS TO POSSESS YOU WITH PURPOSE!

The dictionary defines possessed as "being influenced or controlled by something"[28] (as an evil spirit, a passion, or an idea). Jesus wants to birth His plans and destiny inside of you in such a way that your purpose consumes every part of your being.

One of my favorite stories in the Bible is the story of the demoniac in Mark 5. Jesus and the disciples cross the Sea of Galilee to the region of the Gerasenes. When they get out of the boat, a man with an evil spirit comes out from the tombs to meet them. The Bible says that nobody can contain this man, even with chains and shackles, because he is so strong that he'd snap and smash the chains. Night and day, he wanders the tombs, howling and cutting himself with sharp stones. The whole city knows who he is. He comes running to Jesus and falls at his feet, shouting, "Jesus,

---

28   "Definition of Possessed." *Merriam-Webster Dictionary.* https://www.merriam-webster.com/dictionary/possessed.

what do you want with me?" Jesus asks the man what his name is. He replies, "My name is Legion." This is the same term used to describe a legion of Roman soldiers—meaning six thousand men. Now *that* is a lot of demons!

This doesn't intimidate Jesus, however, because He knows His identity. He knows who He is! Jesus casts the demons out into a herd of pigs, and the pigs run down the steep bank and drown. The man is completely set free! The next day, the former demon-possessed man is sitting in the town center with Jesus, fully clothed and in his right mind. What those town people say still makes me scratch my head. Instead of celebrating what Jesus did, they're afraid and plead with Jesus to leave their region!

How did these people see the miracle of Jesus and yet not want Him around? **Today's culture is, likewise, more comfortable with the demonic than the divine. People can handle being around the filth of culture, but seeing someone's life being changed by Jesus—they can't stomach it.** This culture can watch shows and movies that are fear-based, that glorify sex, and that are violent, perverted, and disgusting. The culture can scroll through pornographic images, hateful posts, lies, gossip, and profanity. But even *mention* the Bible, healing, prayer, purity, or Jesus, and the culture freaks out. Think about it: Mark 5 tells the story of a human being restored to his right mind, speaking truth, living the way God designed him to live—and his culture wanted nothing to do with the healer.

In fact, many Christians are more comfortable around lies than they are around the truth! Let's take this further: Many of your friends are okay with the old you—the you that partied, felt depressed, lived in fear, was addicted to substances or porn, and had a filthy mouth. But they have a problem with the new you—the saved, changed, and free you. These kinds of friends want you to keep that to yourself, or else they don't want to be around you. As soon as you start to talk about being set free, they change the subject or dismiss it.

God's presence challenges our comfort. In the last chapter, we addressed bondage and what holds us back from freedom. One such type of bondage is comfort. We, as humans, like to feel comfortable. It's safe, easy, and it feels good. **Our flesh would rather be comforted than crucified.** Comfort, however, is a counterfeit to the presence of God. The Bible says the Holy Spirit is our Comforter. **The presence of the Holy Spirit confronts our comfort and challenges us to change.** The former demoniac wanted to get into the boat with Jesus after he'd been healed—he wanted to stay where he would feel safe and comfortable. The last thing this man wanted to do was face the people who knew the *old* him. That would require stepping out of his comfort zone.

Your comfort is in conflict with your faith. You don't have to understand everything God is trying to do. God did not give you faith to *understand* Him—He gave you faith to live victoriously, trusting in Him! God's presence births purpose into our hearts. When the former demoniac obeyed Jesus and stayed in his hometown, the news of Jesus spread like wildfire. Everyone knew the undeniable truth of this man's healing—that Jesus was the Messiah—and many chose to put their faith in Him! Years later, the Romans were persecuting the Jews. In 70 A.D., they destroyed the temple in Jerusalem. The Jews scattered. Followers of Jesus needed a safe haven. Where did massive numbers of them go? The Decapolis region—the very place that this former demoniac had evangelized!

Jesus had a plan. The former demoniac prepared a way to protect a future generation from persecution. Jesus turned his pain into his purpose. His past became a platform of redemption. Jesus took a man possessed with demons and possessed him with his purpose! There is purpose in your pain.

Maybe you're Christian who isn't feeling fulfilled—maybe you want to become possessed with purpose but something is holding you back. Let me ask you this: is your comfort in competition with your calling? Your comfort *must* be crucified with Christ, or else it will continue to hinder your calling. Jesus wants to use your story for His purpose—to touch a generation! But you won't find out what this purpose looks like until you let go of your comfort.

ENCOUNTERING HIS PRESENCE

No matter what's blocking us from our purpose—sin, doubt, complacency, or even a lack of motivation to spend daily time with God—we need an encounter with God in order to move forward. The demoniac encountered the presence of Jesus and received his identity, power, and purpose. Likewise, we won't receive these things until we get into God's presence. An encounter with Him is what changes everything. How do we encounter Him? Simply by being still and talking to Him! Worship Him. Tell Him you love Him. Express to Him how much you want to know Him—how much you need Him. He will respond. Ask Him to fill you with His presence, set you free, and lead you into the purpose for which He created you.

Encountering Jesus may begin with repenting and asking for forgiveness for those sins, those things holding you back from Him—even the grudges against others (believers, the church, and so on) that you're harboring in your heart. The word "repent" literally means to turn from sin, feel regret, and to change one's mind. When we truly surrender everything to Him—our way of thinking and living—then we will encounter His presence and experience His power. We will never be the same.

It's worth mentioning here that there's a distinct difference between the presence of God and the power of God (or, put another way, the glory of God and the anointing of God). Many in Christian circles use these words interchangeably; for our purposes, we'll use the words "presence" for glory and "power" for anointing. Understanding this distinction is important to grasping the truth of what God's presence does in our lives.

God's presence is *Him*. God's power is *what comes with Him*. His presence stills you. His power strengthens you. We seek God's presence so that we can live in God's power. Claudio Freidzon, one of the greatest modern-day revivalists from Argentina, says, "God's power reveals what God does. God's presence reveals who God is."[29] We seek His presence, not His power—because the latter automatically comes with the former!

Here's another lens through which to look at it: God's presence is for *us* so that we may know Him. However, His power is so that *others* may know Him *through us*. His presence changes us to be more like Christ on the *inside* so that we are empowered to live more like Christ on the *outside*.

One time, when Debi wanted a cereal box that was high up in the pantry, she became frustrated after she failed to climb up to reach it on her own and cried out for me: "Daddy, help!"

I walked into the kitchen, picked her up, and grabbed the box for her. "Debi, all you had to do was ask me for help." My presence brought the power to grab the

---

29   "Claudio Freidzon + Jeremy Riddle + Steffany Gretzinger | Jesus '19." *YouTube*. Uploaded December 29, 2019. https://www.youtube.com/watch?v=7yqv2KCjvGM.

cereal box. When we have Jesus' presence, His power automatically comes with it. **His presence empowers you to live out His purpose.**

A RELATIONSHIP—NOT A RELIGION

Encountering Jesus' presence is about embracing a relationship with Him. Christianity is about relationship—about a continuous encounter with God; religion is about striving to live by principles apart from that relationship! Religion is trying to live devoted to God without a living encounter with God! This is why we must fall in love with Jesus. When He touches your life, you'll discover how real He is, and you'll spend the rest of your life wanting to serve him!

Sin originally separated us from God's presence; now, it's God's presence that separates us from sin! Jesus separated the demoniac from his past, which empowered him to step into his purpose. It's the same for us today. Jesus didn't die just to get you into heaven; He died to get heaven into you! He is passionately in love with you and desires to fill you so that you can live every day of your life to the fullest. The hardest thing isn't being filled with the Spirit of God but being emptied of yourself—letting go of your mistakes, past sins, and the tendency to do things your way. When we empty ourselves, we make room for more of Him. We become consumed with His presence, able to move in power and to impact others.

All purpose begins in His presence. It's where dead things come to life, the sick are healed, hope is restored, sin is forgiven. It's where every storm is stilled, freedom is found, sin and shame are stripped. It's in encountering Jesus that our every need is met—and everything changes.

MICHELLE'S STORY

Screaming at the top of her lungs, the girl fell to the ground, shaking violently. This was the scene before me one night in Belgium, as a young woman encountered the power of God's love. It was as if somebody were trying to light her on fire. I didn't know what was going on, or why she spontaneously reacted to my altar call.

I'd just finished speaking at a youth camp, and now found myself preaching to a group of young adults in an amazing local church. The main demographic were twenty-somethings from Congo who lived in Belgium. I shared my story of brokenness, freedom, and purpose. When the altar time came, I simply said, "If you're ready to find freedom and encounter the presence of Jesus, come to the front."

As soon as I uttered these words, this young lady began wailing loudly, like she was in pain. I looked at the crowd and said, "Well, this just got real very quickly!"

Immediately, everyone gathered around this woman to pray like they were going to cast out demons. I got her to quiet down, and asked her to stand back up to talk calmly with me. I asked what her name was and what she was feeling. She shared how she felt an intense pain pushing on her chest—like she couldn't breathe. Most people started praying intensely. However, I walked away for a moment, asking the Lord what was happening. The Holy Spirit gently impressed upon me that she had been sexually violated as a young girl and was dealing with shame and rejection. I walked back and asked the young woman if she wanted Jesus to touch every area of her life—to be free. She could barely talk, but whispered, "Yes."

I told her what the Lord had showed me, and that, tonight God was setting her free. She started shaking uncontrollably again, screaming at the top of her lungs. She fell to her knees. I knew God was touching her. I continued to pray over her for another few minutes until, all of a sudden, the Holy Spirit gently touched her, and she fell back and collapsed to the ground.

After several minutes of being on the ground, the woman got up, and it was as if she were a new person! The pain in her chest was gone. The screaming stopped. The look in her eyes and her countenance changed. She shared how she had encountered Jesus and had felt the love of God wash away all the shame, rejection, and pain. What I didn't know is that the pastor of that church and his wife had prayed for a divine set-up that night. They knew I was coming, and that this girl wasn't welcomed in several churches in their area. Every time praise and worship started, Michelle would start screaming. The pastors didn't know how to handle her or what to do. So they just asked her to leave.

Michelle had been raped as a child, and had been involved sexually with a deacon in another church. Her dad had died of AIDS on her second birthday. She was carrying an extreme amount of pain, shame, and unforgiveness. It was like a modern-day "woman caught in adultery" story. The pastor and his wife had heard about how God moves through me in services and said, "Let's get her here and see what Jesus will do tonight!" Had I known this in advance, I may not have wanted her to show up, either! But a one-night encounter with Jesus changed her destiny!

I know you may be thinking, *Tim, that's a little extreme isn't it? Can this really happen? How do you know she was changed?* I'm glad you asked! The very next year, I went back to Belgium to speak at a different youth conference. Guess who I ran into? Yep, it was Michelle. She was serving as a youth leader at the camp, mentoring girls! She was totally changed and full of the joy of Jesus! Three years later, she was getting her bachelor's degree in education, she was a part of the church's worship team, and she was leading the prayer team of the church! She had once been possessed by pain, but is now possessed with purpose.

God's presence puts you on a new path and gives you new purpose. His presence is where your mission becomes bigger than your mistakes! In His presence, your nature changes. Your taste for sin evaporates. When I encountered the love and presence of Jesus, it changed my desires. The old party spots and clubs were no longer desirable. I was ready to receive His purpose for me. What do you need to be separated from to make room for who you are becoming and what you are called to do?

PURPOSE IS NOT A PLAN—IT'S A PERSON

I remember when I first went to see an experienced counselor named Nelson Alsup. He's now been a mentor and spiritual advisor in my life for the past twenty years. The reason I went to see him was because I wanted God's plan and purpose for my life, but I couldn't seem to find it. During my time of searching, Nelson had me do some spiritual gifting assessments and even sent me to the local community college for a battery of tests. These tests looked at problem-solving skills, motor skills, language, reading, and math to discover a person's strengths. Based on your results, they'd match you up to potential career options.

While this was all helpful, it still didn't solve my problem. Nothing in the list they gave me jumped out to me. It wasn't inaccurate; it was simply information in my head—it didn't click in or stir my heart. I needed to be moved emotionally—to feel like my life would make an impact in the world!

Why is encountering Jesus so vital to finding purpose? **Purpose is not a plan. It is a person!** Purpose isn't found in a program, a plan, a curriculum, or even a bunch of practical how-tos. The demoniac we studied earlier didn't receive his mission first—he encountered Jesus first. Purpose is a byproduct—the overflow—of a Jesus encounter. You can't separate purpose from His presence. There is no purpose aside from Him. The good news is that He promises believers that we will always have His presence: Matthew 28:20 says, "And surely I am with you always, to the very end of the age."

There's recently been a huge movement in the body of Christ towards being purpose-driven. In fact, the second most-purchased book after the Bible is Rick Warren's *The Purpose-Driven Life*. While I align personally with Warren's writings, **I believe God is shifting us from being "purpose-driven" to being "presence-driven."** Of course, we need to be focused on our purpose, but our *primary* focus should be on His presence. Our world is rapidly changing—our economy, sickness and disease, pandemics, technology—all of the areas of our society are dynamic. If we don't stay focused on His presence, we will miss the very thing He's saying to us in a critical season, causing us to miss our practical purpose in that season!

If you're graduating this year, or if you've just graduated and are looking for a new job or career, you have a lot of options in front of you. The goal is not to pick the "best one," but to seek the Source who can help you choose. Instead of idolizing the plan, worship Jesus Himself. All through Scripture, we read about people who met Jesus and whose lives were radically changed. His very presence overcame natural laws. He healed blind eyes, opened deaf ears, restored paralytics and lepers, cast demons out of people, forgave people of their sins, and raised people from the dead. He spoke to violent storms, and the winds became still. He caused food to multiply to feed five thousand people. Everywhere He went, the people who genuinely wanted to encounter Him were transformed forever. When they encountered Jesus, He gave them a new plan, a new purpose.

Jesus is the goal. Too many times in Christian circles, people are chasing miracles, breakthroughs, purposes, their next step or met needs. These things in themselves aren't wrong; the priorities have just been reversed. When we seek Jesus, we will find Him and His purpose for our lives. Matthew 6:33 (ESV) says, "Seek first the kingdom of God and his righteousness, and all these things will be added to you."

Everyone quotes Jeremiah 29:11 (ESV): "For I know the plans I have for you, declares the Lord, plans for welfare and not for evil, to give you a future and a hope." However, few quote the most important piece of that chapter, which is verses 12-13: "Then you will call upon me and come and pray to me, and I will hear you. You will seek me and find me, when you seek me with all your heart." If you want to be who God is calling you to be, you must prioritize the Person, not the plan. You will find Him when you seek Him with your whole heart. This is the prerequisite to finding His plans, because **His plans are revealed in His presence!**

If you want to be who God is calling you to be, you must prioritize the Person, not the plan. So many are looking for direction in their careers and feel frustrated, not knowing what to do. They talk with friends, mentors, or even a counselor like I did, but nothing seems to work. Nobody seems to have answers. Maybe that's the whole point! God may be using this dissatisfaction in your life to cause you to seek Him diligently, for He alone has the answers and knows what you need. Just maybe, He wants His presence to be enough—to be your main desire. When His presence becomes your pursuit, that's when He reveals His plans!

WHERE'S DADA?

When my kids were little, we used to play a game they loved called "Where's Dada?" This is our version of Hide and Go Seek. I'd hide somewhere in the house; they'd count and try to find me. It might be in a closet, in a shower, on top of the washer or dryer, or under the covers of a bed.

When they couldn't find me, I'd wait until they were in another room and yell, "Where's Dada?" Their little feet would come scurrying across the tile floor. Their giggles were priceless as they anticipated finding me. I remember hearing their little voices talking to each other: "Shhh. I think I heard him. He's over here."

"No, I think he's in the bathroom, or hiding in the closet."

Those little, squeaky toddler voices were so cute. I always had to cover my mouth with a pillow, shirt, or my hand to avoid laughing. Sometimes, I couldn't help it. There was always a genuine explosion of laughter as they found me. Every time they discovered my hiding place, I would yell, "There's Dada!"

Sometimes, I'd tell the kids that I had a surprise for them, but they'd have to find me first. After we were done, I'd say, "Okay, because you found me, I'm also going to let you have pizza, lie in Mommy and Daddy's bed, and watch a movie with us." They didn't chase after me because I had something for them—they simply loved the joy of finding me. **The joy of pursuing Jesus is the purpose of living. Discovering the plan or treat waiting for you is just a bonus.** Finding Jesus is the purpose of life; all the other things we get to do for Him are just bonuses.

YOU CAN ENCOUNTER JESUS ANYWHERE, IN ANY WAY!

Jesus doesn't always encounter us the same way. It's not about a certain song being played or being at a specific church location or service. There's no set method to encountering Jesus. I've encountered the presence of God at church services, during individual prayer time, while surfing, on the soccer field, and during one-on-one conversations. You can encounter Him in your room, in a church, in your car, outside, on a sports field, or in a coffee shop. In fact, I've had dozens of young people cry in a coffee shop as the Holy Spirit touched their lives during a conversation or counseling time.

Have you ever had a conversation with someone that stirred your heart with hope—that left you wanting more of what they had? Even after you leave these conversations, you find yourself thinking about something the person said or how you felt when you were around them. Their passion for Jesus, their hope, their joy or their purpose is contagious. If you need an encounter with God, spend time with people who are encountering God. It doesn't have to be a set place; just connect with Jesus-loving people. It will stir your heart to want more of Him. You may just encounter Him!

EVAN'S STORY

I met Tim—I know him as Coach Tim—when he started showing up at soccer practice my junior year of high school. I had a handful of interactions with Coach Tim, but we hadn't had any conversation deeper than what I needed on the soccer field.

After a few weeks, he asked me after practice if we could connect sometime—he had something to share with me. From what I had seen of Coach

Tim so far, he seemed like a really encouraging guy, so I agreed right away. What was there to lose? Getting on a coach's good side never hurt anyone.

We met a few days later at Starbucks. I'm not sure I'd even grown fond of coffee yet, but Tim was a cool guy, and it seemed like the mature way to hang out. The meeting itself was reminiscent of a meeting I'd had with a mental health counselor not long before—at the exact same Starbucks, actually. We grabbed an outside table and warmed up our conversation with jokes and soccer stories.

When these topics died down, Tim revealed an 8x11 sheet of white printer paper with a paragraph or two typed out. He explained that, right when he met me, before we'd really spoken at all, God gave him a word—a picture may be a better description—of my life's circumstances. Tim had seen a man dressed in a military uniform, wanting to lead and serve, but sitting in a closet hiding. He also saw a doctor bringing healing to many people. He didn't know anything about my life or my family, but God allowed Coach Tim to essentially "read my mail."

My father has made a career out of military service; my mother is a doctor. I was a depressed, frustrated man who wanted to be a leader but couldn't break free of the chains holding me down. At that time, I was relying on medication to help regulate my moods and emotions due to my depression. Get this: I had an understanding of God. In fact, I could passionately teach the "theology" of Christianity and why it works. I could academically debate in favor of God's existence and the point of life. But what Coach Tim had just done, by listening to the Holy Spirit, blew my mind. How could someone know so many things about me that I hadn't shared with anyone? It brought so many questions to my mind. Was I just under-standing God but not experiencing His power? I believe, at that time, the answer was YES.

Coach Tim and I talked for hours about God, how His Son, Jesus', sacrifice made a way for us to access communion with the Holy Spirit, how we have access to the power of the Spirit, and how God wanted to use us to enact His perfect, miracle-filled plan. That night, I went home fired up, excited by what God had revealed to me. I was so excited that I decided to pray a dangerous prayer. I laid down, pulled up my blankets, and asked God to show me something I could hold onto for the rest of my life: something that would be irrefutable evidence that He is alive and active. To me, it was a casual prayer. I didn't really expect anything in particular.

I woke up in the middle of the night, trembling with fear, eyes tightly shut. I was clearly awake, but the fear that gripped me prevented me from opening my eyes, moving, or saying anything. The right side of my body, head to toe, felt extremely hot. I had the sense that someone was leaning over me with their face extremely close to mine. I heard a scratchy, high-pitched voice say, "What are you doing here?"

At first, I thought the evil voice was talking to me; I realized it was speaking across me, to something or someone on my right side. My left side felt cool and calm. I lay there with the understanding—which I'd gained earlier that day at Starbucks—that the Holy Spirit gave me the power to command evil spirits. I tried to speak out, but my voice caught in my throat. I croaked. Eyes still shut, feeling afraid, I was finally able to yell out loud, "Get out of here!"

My body immediately cooled all over. I felt a wave of calm wash away the fear and trembling. I was finally able to open my eyes after what felt like a few hours. I realized that the voice that said, "What are you doing here?" was speaking to the Holy Spirit, or an angel, that was with me on my left side. After that experience, I was utterly convinced that I would never doubt the existence of my God.

The following day, I stopped taking my depression medication. I believed God had healed my depression. He did. I never took that medication again! Since then, my passion for Christ has continued to grow. During my senior year, I went with Coach Tim and three other soccer players on a three-day cruise, on which we went through the Purpose Curriculum. It was extremely helpful. What specifically altered the course of my life was creating my personal purpose statement. It took three days of actively talking and developing the thought, but I finally landed on it: "I exist to lead and run with an army of people, warriors, to crush the enemy in the *pursuit of Jesus." I also realized that, at an even more basic level, I exist to LOVE people to the best of my ability.*

God continued to guide my steps. Now, I work for Action Church in Orlando, Florida, directing our student ministry. I've gotten the opportunity to help children, middle school students, and high school students develop their own personal purpose statements that I pray they are able to lean on for decades to come. Looking back, I would have been a pretty poor life planner for myself. Thank God that He has a plan for our lives!

This story still chokes me up. I knew Evan when he was a high schooler, dealing with doubt and depression, feeling alone. Now, he is impacting hundreds of students on a weekly basis. He found purpose!

Two things were key to Evan's transformation: First he had an encounter with Jesus where he transitioned from having an "understanding" about who God is, to experiencing His presence and power. This was when everything changed. Secondly, after three days of going through our purpose curriculum, Evan finally discovered what his purpose was. What a powerful truth this is! When you experience the presence of Jesus, He changes you, gives you purpose, and then, as a byproduct, reveals His plan.

It's when you come into contact with Jesus that you become alive to who you have been called to be and what you have been called to do. In order to find purpose, you must prioritize the Person, not the plan. There *is* no true purpose outside of Christ! In order to become who God is calling you to be, you must make seeking Him your greatest priority.

When was the last time you were desperate for God? When did you last cry uncontrollably in His presence? When did you last feel His love and peace flood your heart? When were your thoughts and emotions consumed by Him last? It's in these encounters that He changes you, becomes so real to you. It's in these moments that you realize everything that matters—all that is eternal—comes from him. Life is no longer about you.

Jesus' presence will birth His purpose in your heart. Find Him, and the plan will be revealed. Diligently seek Him, and He will empower you to live out the reason you exist. It's what happened to the demoniac. It's what happened to me and what I have seen happen to thousands of others. Now, it's your turn. Jesus is waiting for you. Go encounter His presence, and become possessed with purpose!

QUESTIONS FOR SELF-REFLECTION

How do you feel about the idea that God wants to "possess you with purpose"? Is there any part of this idea that excites you? Is there any part of this idea that troubles or confuses you?

_____

_____

_____

_____

In your own words, how would you differentiate between the presence of God and the power of God? Can you think of any down-to-earth examples of how they are distinct?

_____

_____

_____

_____

How would it change the way you live and pursue your purpose if you lived every day knowing that it wasn't a plan or a place, but a Person?

_____

_____

_____

_____

Are there any action steps you feel called to take as you complete this chapter?

CHAPTER 6

THE CROSSROADS OF PURPOSE

I remember reaching a major crossroads when I was twenty-nine years old. I'd just been in a car accident and totaled my vehicle. I'd recently lost my job, drained my bank accounts, and liquidated my mutual fund to survive. I was broke and desperate. In the middle of a hot Florida summer, I took an outdoors painting job from my stepdad, who's a general contractor. The job paid $1,000 for the week—it barely paid the bills. It was, literally, a week from hell. I felt like Jonah in the Bible, on the run, in denial. I cussed more that week than any other time in my life. I knew that I had to make a choice.

A crossroads is an intersection where decisions are made. Serious, life-altering mistakes can happen. If you make a wrong turn, you can become severely lost or get headed in the wrong direction. This was the most critical season of my life; how I navigated this intersection would either lead me to or away from my purpose. I knew my life needed to change, but I didn't know where to begin, how to figure things out, or what questions to ask. I needed some practical guidance and application of spiritual truth. This wrestling led me to create this material.

Have you ever been to a new mall you weren't familiar with and felt frustrated that you couldn't find a store? Maybe you didn't even know what stores were inside the mall. Then, you came across a big sign or screen with a map of the entire place—every store listed for your convenience. In the middle of the map, you see that glorious red arrow and the words "You Are Here." You breathe a sigh of relief. Finally—some answers. **It's those sacred words, "You Are Here," that keep you from wandering aimlessly and losing your mind.** They allow you to see where you are in relation to where you're heading.

You are standing in the middle of the intersection at a crossroads. You may feel stuck or frustrated, just like I did, and not know where to begin. You may just be looking for what's next. I needed practical tools to help me pray, inventory my life, and know what was available to me. The rest of this material is focused on helping you take inventory of your life and discover your options. It will continue to build on the spiritual foundation we've laid so far. These principles are intended to give you a road map to discovering your practical purpose.

As you begin to ask yourself the right questions, and become aware of how the different areas of your life can work together according to God's plan, your purpose will come more and more into focus. I wish somebody had shown me this stuff twenty years ago—it would have changed everything!

TAKING INVENTORY

Your purposes are already in you! Just like in the bucket and well metaphor we shared in a previous chapter. Proverbs 20:5 says, "The purposes of a person's heart are deep waters, but one who has insight draws them out." We want to draw out your deep purposes. The process we've developed has helped hundreds of teens, college students, and twenty-somethings find their purpose. Now, it's your turn.

Successful businesses take inventory of their products. It's a key part of knowing what sizes, colors, styles, or flavors sell the best—what makes the most money— what's in stock—what needs to be ordered. Taking inventory of your life will help you maximize your life's purpose and live abundantly. How do we do it? By looking at multiple areas of your life in order to gain a clearer perspective and understand what your life offers to the world. This process can be tedious and tiresome, but it's absolutely necessary. There are many websites, programs, books, and institutions dedicated to this—all of them have their own systems. This book is based on a system I believe is both simple and biblical. It's a starting point; you can add on other systems should you choose to. There's no limit to self-discovery!

CAREER AND CALLING

When I first started youth ministry, I was selling life insurance from a rented bedroom. Then, I switched to working for my mom and stepdad's construction company, running job sites and doing public relations. I was much more suited for the latter than painting or physical labor. While working at the construction company, I earned good pay and was able to still follow my call to youth ministry. Still, I felt that my career and calling were both meant to be in youth ministry. It wasn't until two years later that I began to be paid for ministry work.

The biggest complaint I hear from young adults is, "I don't know how to make a living at what I feel called to do." Many want to make money doing something they're passionate about and feel called to; however, this isn't always immediately the case. When your current career seems to be separating you from your calling, frustration and friction set in.

Your career is what you are paid for; your calling is what you were made for. These were the words God spoke to me back in 2009, during a rough financial period of life. Your calling is what you were created to do—how you impact the world. Your career is the practical way God provides for your life during that season. These can change over time; however, they are both intrinsic parts of living out your practical purpose. When career and calling intersect; when you get paid for what you feel called to do, you are in what I call your "sweet spot."

You may be a business owner, have a job, and make a lot of money, but what's the *purpose* of that money? Your career empowers you to live out your calling. You're a full-time missionary masquerading as a doctor, a business owner, a musician, a teacher, or whatever career you choose. Your career allows you to put resources, time, and finances into your calling. Being a businessman allows you the money to help underprivileged kids; being a teacher allows you to mentor teenagers. Being a doctor gives you the ability to help the poor for free. God has given you the ability to make money not just for yourself but to serve others in your purpose.

One of the biggest challenges in living out your purpose is in the dichotomy of following your passions while being able to make money. It can be hard to find the balance. God wants to meet your needs, and sometimes this may require you to stay the course until He makes it possible to live out both your career and your calling. However, at other times, you'll be able to do both in the same role.

JOB VS. CAREER

According to Nelson Alsup, "The main reason people don't have purpose is they have a satisfaction with the status quo. People settle for a job instead of a career. They get a paycheck, cash it, and buy the necessities. It meets their basic needs, but it doesn't bring life and fulfillment." Alsup believes this is similar to Stockholm Syndrome, in which captives develop an affection for and loyalty toward their abusers. It basically boils down to being a survival tactic. In order to survive, one finds a way to adapt.

While there may be seasons of life in which you have to simply get by, God didn't call you to merely survive. He called you to thrive! **In a job, you work to get by; a career, on the other hand, has the potential to become something bigger.** If you're working at a fast-food restaurant, unless you have a plan to go into management, you're just working a job. You're better off finding something you enjoy in order to work towards building a career. You owe it to yourself to make intentional plans toward a career that you will enjoy. Knowing your personal identity and practical purpose will help you do just that.

How do you determine the career you're meant to pursue—the calling for which you're created? This is where personal identity and practical purpose collide! This is the essence of the Purpose Cross.

THE PURPOSE CROSS

The cross is the most iconic symbol in Christianity. When most people see it, they have an immediate understanding of what it means. A few years ago, God showed me how all the complex ideas around purpose can be clearly applied and communicated through this symbol. These principles of purpose overlay on the cross like a four-way highway. Purpose is found at the intersection of these four paths. They intersect in the middle, right where Jesus' heart was. It is here, in the middle, where God's priorities and our unique design collide! These ideas point to the core purpose of your life.

Each of us comes to a crossroad of decision when it comes to what we want to do with our lives. On the road to purpose, there are signs and mile markers that help point you in the right direction. The Purpose Cross includes your personal identity, practical purpose, and spiritual purpose. As you take inventory of your life, you'll begin to see how each road intersects with the others. These four roads meet in the middle—the intersection where "The Heart of God" and "Your Divine Design" collide, causing an explosion of purpose.

The cross is both vertical and horizontal. The vertical component represents our relationship with God. The horizontal component represents our relationship with others. Both of these are key in fulfilling your purpose. If you don't have both working in unity, your purpose will be incomplete.

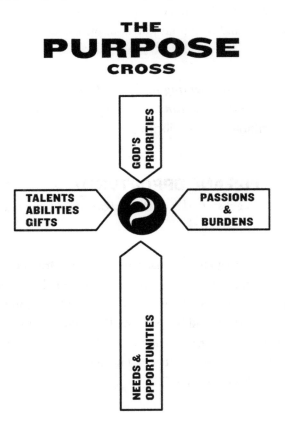

THE
PURPOSE
CROSS

GOD'S PRIORITIES

TALENTS
ABILITIES
GIFTS

PASSIONS
&
BURDENS

NEEDS &
OPPORTUNITIES

SECTION 1: GOD'S PRIORITIES ON EARTH

Discovering our purpose begins with knowing God's priorities and purposes on earth. God already gave us key commands and priorities to live out. We need to ask ourselves some questions: *What's most important to Him? What are His main concerns on earth? What does He want to accomplish?* These are the priorities in heaven that flow down to the earth, to the middle intersection of the Purpose Cross.

First and foremost, Jesus took all 613 religious laws in the Jewish law, the Torah, and boiled them down to two ideas: loving God and loving others (Matthew 22:37-40). Secondly, He calls believers to make disciples (Matthew 28:18-20). Throughout the New Testament, Jesus continuously gave instructions to preach the gospel, heal the sick, and cast out demons. God's priority on earth is to communicate His love in everything, to everyone. He wants us to take care of widows and orphans, feed the poor, help the brokenhearted, and set the captives free. Whether it's helping a homeless person, working in a corporate office, being on a sports field, or working on a job site, we are to be Jesus' ambassadors. His priorities involve demonstrating and living out kingdom principles on earth, so others are drawn to Him.

Ask yourself: *What is God wanting to do on the earth right now? What is He breathing upon right now? How can I attach myself to it?* Whatever you do with your life must incorporate God's priorities.

SECTION 2: NEEDS AND OPPORTUNITIES

"The best way to get started is to stop talking about and begin doing."
—Walt Disney

One Saturday, I felt led to go to a ministry breakfast in Orlando. I'd been reading a few books by Dr. Mike Murdock, a guy I saw often on TV. He was a little controversial to some; nevertheless, he was in town, and I felt compelled to attend. During breakfast, Murdock and his protégé, Dr. Dave Martin, talked about the force of God's favor. I wanted this favor. I wanted to fulfill the purpose for which I was created. I didn't know where to begin. I needed a starting point. I needed that red arrow that said, "You Are Here!"

After the breakfast, I went up to Dave. My heart was beating out of my chest. I felt God stirring me to make a decision. But how would I *know* if I was supposed to finally say yes to being my dad's youth pastor? It was the very thing he'd asked me about for seven years—the very thing I'd said no to. I asked Dave a simple question: "How did you know that God was calling you into the ministry?"

I expected this profound answer—for the trumpet of God to sound from heaven, or a glowing light to shine on his face as he answered me. It was the exact opposite. Dave said, "It started by me just filling a need. I saw a need, and I filled it."

The weight of his words was like a sledgehammer to my heart. I almost burst into tears on the spot. *Fill a need?* Dad had been asking me for years to do this very thing, but I hadn't been able to see it, because my heart wasn't ready. I wasn't walking in freedom. Now, I saw it clearly. The need I was being called to fill became clear. I took a deep breath, swallowed, and said, "Wow, thank you. That's all I needed to hear."

As I walked out of the room, I saw Mike Murdock heading towards the elevator with his security guard. I ran after him and caught him before he got into the elevator. Nowadays, I probably would have been tackled or met at gunpoint by his security guard. I said, "Dr. Mike, I've got to tell you what God spoke to me today." This time, I did burst into tears. I don't know if he understood a word I said, but I shared how God had spoken to me about His call on my life for youth ministry—that I'd been running from it for seven years, but that I'd finally made a decision to answer that call.

Filling a need may become your life's seed. It really is that simple. Find a need and fill it. **I didn't realize how one act of obedience could change my destiny. What once was an "I will *never* do that" role became my full-blown passion!**

Needs and opportunities are God's earthly purposes that He allows you to see. These priorities begin on earth and point us toward heavenly priorities—converging at the middle of the Purpose Cross. What opportunities are around you? What needs can you fill? What opportunities for new experiences has God brought to you? The answers that present themselves may be the very ones God is asking you to obediently step into this season. Let me give you a hint: If there's a need that keeps resurfacing, even when you've tried to ignore it, it's a clue to your purpose. It may or may not be something you're passionate about—it may be a simple act of obedience that blossoms into something greater. We will discuss more fully in the next chapter how needs and opportunities are a part of God's purpose process, and how they guide you.

When opportunity knocks, don't complain about the noise! Don't complain about the pay, the time invested, the inconvenience or the sacrifice made. Be open and thankful, because you never know where one will lead. Don't stay stagnant. Stop waiting. Get moving.

SECTION 3: T.A.G.–TALENTS, ABILITIES, AND GIFTS

Do you remember playing the game "tag" as a kid? This game is timeless. You touch someone, yell, "You're it!" and run. The person who's "it" chases others to tag someone else, who then becomes "it." There are some foundational rules that apply. For example, no tag backs. You can't tag someone immediately after they tag you. Most times, there's a designated "base" where you're safe. Some kids even cheat when they're about to be tagged by calling any object close to them "base."

When kids don't play the game correctly, it's boring—it loses its excitement, and arguments can even break out. When tagged, kids sometimes quit or walk around slowly, like they didn't want to play. The reason kids quit is because they lack the confidence to be "it!" They can't catch anyone—or they're afraid to try. When played correctly, tag can lead to endless laughter and excitement—it keeps you on your toes.

I remember playing tag as a kid. I still play it as a dad with my kids. After a while of my kids not being able to catch me, I slow down and let them. I even love being it! I love the challenge, but also the screams of the kids as I chase them over couches, around tables, and through bedrooms. I love hearing them giggle and laugh.

In the same way, **God has tagged you with His talents, abilities, and gifts. He's placed everything you need to fulfill your purpose inside of you.** He has called you to be "IT." God wants you to use your T.A.G. to reach others. Your T.A.G. puts you on the third road of purpose. When your unique talents, abilities, and gifts collide with the other roads on the Purpose Cross—when they are used effectively—you will make a mark on the world like nobody else can.

Talents, abilities, and gifts are those God-given things you're naturally good at. They are things that come easily to you. In *Discover Your Strengths* by Marcus Buckingham and Donald O. Clifton, the authors state that every person is capable of doing something better than the next ten thousand people. They call this area the "strength zone." Working within your talents is key to fulfilling your purpose.

As a kid, I loved playing soccer. I'd play outside for hours. My parents always said I had a natural ability for the sport. Although I worked hard at developing my skills, it was evident that I had a knack for it. Soccer helped me learn how to lead and connect with people. I've also always been naturally gifted at influencing and speaking to people. When I was a teenager, I was the person many of my friends came to for advice—the person with whom they shared their problems. I discovered that I was good at listening and applying practical wisdom to their situations. Listening came easily for me. I didn't have to work at it, and I could do it for hours. It didn't drain me; instead, it refueled me. Later in life, through a few different jobs, I also discovered I was good at sales. I was naturally talented and comfortable in front of a room.

Even though I can see it clearly now, back then, I had no idea that all of these talents would collide on these crossroads of purpose. I didn't know I would become a counselor, youth speaker, and soccer coach. When I laid down my agenda, God was able to take my natural talents and use them for His glory. Up until then, I'd merely used them for my own purposes. Now, I was using them for His.

So what are you naturally good at? What are the things you do that garner the most notice, compliments, and praise? These are the things that come easily to you. God isn't interested just in your natural *ability*—He also wants your *availability*. Will you make your talents and gifts available to God? Are you willing to use them for His glory?

SPIRITUAL T.A.G.

God also tags us with spiritual talents, abilities, and gifts when we become born-again Christians. These are the gifts referred to in 1 Corinthians 12. "Giftings," in a spiritual sense, speak of calling: the spiritual reason you exist and the impact you were created to make. For example, connecting with and encouraging people has always been easy for me. One of my spiritual gifts is the gift of *encouragement.* When I step into using this gift, it has a special impact on people because of the grace God has placed on my life for it.

Your gifts are what give you the ability to fulfill your calling. I would strongly suggest you take some assessments and discover your spiritual gifts as a part of your journey. They'll play an essential role in reinforcing the rest of the Purpose Cross principles.

In 2 Timothy 1, the apostle Paul tells Timothy to fan into flame the gift of God that was placed upon him through the laying on of Paul's hands. Paul had imparted the gifts of God into Timothy's life. During this time, Nero, the emperor of Rome, was persecuting and killing Christians. People all around Timothy were being impacted. He was leading the largest church in that time in Ephesus and was challenged to be courageous in the face of fear. Paul was encouraging Timothy to speak openly, unashamedly, about Christ—to declare the message of the gospel.

The word picture Paul used with Timothy was "fanning into flame" our gifts: stirring them up inside of us. Paul was reminding his protégé that his gifts were already inside him; he just had to choose to use them. Everything Timothy needed was already there, ready to be activated. Your gifts are also inside you. If we want to have an impact in this world, we must discover and utilize both our natural and spiritual gifts!

Natural talents are developed through practice; spiritual giftings are developed through prayer. That is how you fan the flames of purpose inside of you! In both cases, God says, "Tag; you're it!" Now, go tag others and change the world! It's time to stir up the gifts inside you. God is inviting you to take ownership of your life's purpose and declare, "I'm it!"

SECTION 4: PASSIONS AND BURDENS

"There is one quality that one must possess to win, and that is definiteness of purpose, the knowledge of what one wants and a burning desire to possess it."
—Napoleon Hill

Passions and burdens are the final piece of the four-way highway of the Purpose Cross. In order to make decisions at your personal crossroads of purpose, you must inventory your passions and burdens. Dictionary.com defines passion as "any powerful or compelling emotion or feeling"—such as love and hate. A burden is something that weighs on you—grieves you. It compels you and calls you to take action. Passions and burdens bring the physical, emotional, mental, and spiritual fuel to accomplish your purpose. They are the *why* behind it all—God's sign that this is His will for your life.

Passions and burdens are two sides of the same coin. **Most everyone asks you the question, "What do you love?" It's a great question, but it is incomplete. You also need to ask yourself, *What do I hate?*** These two answers are clues to the problem God has called you to solve! For our sake, when I refer to passions, I am referring to what you love. Burdens usually are what weigh on you. What do you hate seeing? What injustices do you feel called to solve? What wrongs do you long to right?

I love soccer, surfing, speaking to young people about purpose, counseling, and helping people discover their purpose and how to break free from dysfunctional patterns of behavior. I hate seeing people who are hopeless, who have no purpose, who are bound up in sin, and who feel lost! These are the same issues, from both sides of the coin. I use my passions to solve a problem in regards to the burdens on my heart for today's generation.

It's important to make a distinction between passion and purpose. My passion follows my purpose, not the other way around. Your passions aren't about you—they point you to your purpose and fuel your motivation to get there. They are fuel for the car, not the car for the fuel.

Think about the story of the Triumphal Entry in Matthew 21: Jesus told His disciples to find a donkey that would be tied up at a certain location. He wanted them to bring the donkey to Him, so He could ride on it, as the Lamb of God, in front of the crowd. The purpose of the donkey wasn't for the donkey. People were crying out to Jesus, "Hosanna!" which means, "Lord, save us!" Imagine the donkey thinking this was about him. That would be ridiculous! The donkey was *for* Jesus, not the other way around.

Just like the donkey, your purpose is to carry and show Jesus to the world! **Your passions and burdens provide strength and emotional fuel for your purpose.** So many put their passions into things that have no eternal value—things that, in five, ten, twenty, or fifty years, nobody will remember or care about. It's time to channel our passions into the right purposes.

So, how do we develop passions and burdens? *Our passions and burdens are shaped by our experiences.* How did I know I loved soccer and surfing? Just by watching them? No! I had to get out there on the field, in the ocean, and experience them. Once I did both at a young age, I was hooked for life! They became my passions.

How did I develop a burden for young people who were lost, hurting, or frustrated about what to do with their lives? I experienced it myself; therefore, it weighs on me and causes me to want to do something about it. Once I got a taste of the impact that counseling and preaching have, I was hooked.

I now use soccer to mentor and lead teen boys to Christ; I use surfing as a mentoring tool and to connect with hard-to-reach kids and share Jesus. I use my passion for speaking, influencing, and listening to others to share the love of Jesus globally. I pray that the diagram of the Purpose Cross becomes your road map. If you're at a crossroads, need to make a big decision, or just feel stuck, this chapter will help you begin to recognize and access the hidden things that have been inside you all along. Inventorying your life will prepare you for stepping into your purpose as you are led by the Lord into your next season.

You may find it hard to identify your passions and burdens, so we have developed a resource to help you. The Purpose Experience Curriculum provides in-depth questions and exercises to get you thinking about everything we've talked about so far. You're not alone on this journey! We're here to help you, and—even better—God is here to coach you every step along the way.

QUESTIONS FOR SELF-REFLECTION

What do you enjoy doing? What kinds of hobbies, interests, or things do you really love?

_____

_____

_____

_____

What natural talents, abilities, and gifts do you possess? These are the things you do better than most around you and are "naturally" good at.

_____

_____

_____

_____

What do you love; what do you hate? These are two sides of the same coin and clues to the problems that God created you to solve.

_____

_____

_____

_____

CHAPTER 7

GOD'S PURPOSE COACHING

In the game of soccer, there are many voices telling you what to do. There are other players on the field, parents, fans, and even referees. Everyone has an opinion of what you should do with the ball, where to pass, what position to be in, where to run, and how to defend. There are constant decisions to be made on the field. Being a coach, I'm constantly reminding my players that the only voices they need to listen to are the coaches'. During playoff games, the crowds get bigger and louder; my team can't hear me across the field. It's during our practices and pregame planning sessions where they get their instructions. That way, when the pressure is on and the crowd is loud, they can confidently execute the game plan.

There's one voice we need to listen to: God's. There will be thousands of voices telling you how to live—negative ones, well-intended ones, and misguided ones. If you listen to these voices, you'll miss what God is saying to you specifically. In order for us to pursue our purpose, we need to hear and know the voice of the Lord for ourselves. **If we want God's results, we must block out the distractions of life and listen to God's voice.**

In this chapter, we're going to uncover the different ways God speaks to us and the key ways in which He reveals His purpose in Scripture. A couple of these concepts were derived from the teachings of Dr. Tim Elmore in his training resource, *A Life of Influence*.[30] Hearing God's voice can seem tricky. People ask me all the time how to do it. My goal for this chapter is two-fold: first, that you will see that God has been speaking to you all along, and second, that you have a clearer understanding of how God leads you into your purpose.

Understanding the key ways God speaks to us is critical to recognizing our purpose. His voice gives direction, and direction guides us to our calling.

THE WAYS GOD SPEAKS

The Bible says that we can know the voice of God. John 10:3-5 says, "The gate-keeper opens the gate for him, and the sheep listen to his voice. He calls his own sheep by name and leads them out. When He has brought out all his own, He goes on ahead of them, and his sheep follow him because they know his voice. But they will never follow a stranger; in fact, they will run away from him because they do not recognize a stranger's voice."

We are God's sheep, and He is our Shepherd. Sheep spend days upon days with their shepherd, and they know his voice. We have the above promise that we, too, can recognize our Shepherd's voice when He speaks to us.

In this section, we'll take a brief look at some of the ways in which God speaks; this isn't a comprehensive list but something to get you thinking and recognizing His voice in your life.

METHOD 1: HIS WORD

The number one way God speaks to us is through His Word. It's His love letter to us. It's His voice. If your Bible is closed, then so is God's mouth. Open up God's mouth, and let Him speak to you. Just as biology is the foundation to becoming a doctor, so the Bible is the foundation to hearing God's voice.

Psalm 119:105 says, "Thy word is a lamp unto my feet and a light to my path." In biblical times, a lamp was a clay pot with a handle that held oil inside. It was kept

---

30 Dr. Tim Elmore. *A Life of Influence: Exploring Your Identity: Sharpening Your Focus.* (Nashville: LifeWay Press, 2004), 8.

in the home, and only had a range of a few feet. It lit up just enough to see the little space in front of you. Each step would move the light forward, and reveal what was in the dark. In the same way, if you don't know what direction to move, God's Word will light the way. After each step, the next step of your purpose is illuminated.

Many people ask me how to hear God's voice, or wonder why He is quiet. My first question is, "Are you opening His mouth and listening? Are you spending time praying?" It's a relationship. He wants to speak to you! So we must make reading His Word a priority. Don't complain that He isn't speaking if your Bible is closed.

METHOD 2: HOLY SPIRIT IMPRESSIONS

The Holy Spirit will give you impressions. He will guide you to take obedient steps of faith. Have you ever had a gut feeling about something? Maybe you felt something inside saying not to go to that party, or date that person, or purchase that item. It was like you could sense it. Then, sure enough, you found out later why you felt that way. It was an inner voice saying, *Be careful*, *Don't do this*, or even simply an inner *knowing* that everything would be okay. Pay attention to those gut feelings. They are signs of the Holy Spirit revealing God's voice in your life.

In the story of Elijah, God spoke to Elijah in a whisper. Elijah had just defeated the prophets of Baal and called down fire from heaven. Because of this, Queen Jezebel wanted him dead. He fled for his life and hid in a cave. God chose to speak to Elijah not through a strong wind, a fire, or an earthquake. He chose to whisper.

God is whispering to us today. The way you hear Him is by being close to Him! It requires being still and quiet. God reveals His secrets for your life when you're desperate to hear Him. Think about it! You only tell secrets to those with whom you're close. When a friend wants to tell you something confidential, they lean into your ear and whisper. Religion yells at you; intimacy whispers to you. God wants us to get close to Him. It's in getting close that you position yourself to hear His secrets.

METHOD 3: VISIONS AND DREAMS

All through Scripture, we see examples of God speaking to people through visions and dreams. God came in this way to Cornelius and Peter, Ezekiel, and Daniel. God speaks to His people by giving them special revelation in visions and dreams—and He can do the same for you and me.

METHOD 4: GODLY RELATIONSHIPS

God also uses relationships to speak to us. These are godly relationships that help us see our blind spots, or that confirm God's voice. They may be with parents, mentors, coaches, teachers, pastors, other spiritual leaders, or godly friends. You can see examples in Scripture, such as Paul's mentorship of Timothy, Moses' guidance of Joshua, or Elijah's leadership of Elisha. Godly relationships help you to recognize the giftings on your life and provide you with an increased sense of direction.

METHOD 5: INNER PEACE

One of the surefire ways to know God's voice is through what I call inner peace. **God is not the author of confusion but of clarity and peace.** This is critical to making decisions and discerning God's voice in a matter. Inner peace is that deep feeling that knows when something is right. Even if it makes no sense in your head, or to people outside, true peace is something unshakable. You know it's from God.

4 KEY WAYS GOD COACHES US INTO OUR PURPOSE

Scripture reveals some key ways in which God coaches us in the process of revealing our purpose. Many times, a combination of the following four ways will be evident, as well. These foundational principles will show up throughout your journey and ultimately lead you to the place God is calling you to be. These aren't just about spiritual direction; they're also related to the practical components of what you do with your life. As you read through this list, look at your life and see how God has been revealing your purpose. Your eyes will be opened as you realize He's been speaking to you all along!

WAY 1: CALL FROM BIRTH

The first way God reveals purpose in Scripture is a call from birth. This is when someone has known their calling since they were young. They always knew God had a specific purpose for them. Many times, this call was validated or confirmed by an adult, parent, pastor, or mentor. While I believe every one of us has a purpose for being born, a call from birth is a situation in which someone is clear on what they want to do from an early age. If his or her parents are believers, then they are aware of it, too.

Examples of the call from birth include Jeremiah, who was called to be a prophet to the nations. Jeremiah 1:5 says, "Before I formed you in the womb I knew you. Before you were born I set you apart; I appointed you as a prophet to the nations." There was also John the Baptist, whose call from birth was to prepare the way for the coming of Jesus. Luke 1:16-17 says, "He will bring back many of the people of Israel to the Lord their God. And he will go on before the Lord, in the spirit and power of Elijah, to turn the hearts of the parents to their children and the disobedient to the wisdom of the righteous—to make ready a people prepared for the Lord."

There was the prophet Samuel, who brought Israel from the period of the judges into establishing God's new form of rule through a monarchy. Samuel's call from birth was to be God's servant. Hannah cried out to God because she was barren. God answered her and gave her a son in 1 Samuel 1:27-28: "'I prayed for this child, and the LORD has granted me what I asked of him. So now I give him to the LORD. For his whole life he will be given over to the LORD.' And he worshiped the LORD there." Samuel was a faithful man, central in the Lord's plans to lead Israel during the end of the judges and into the early era of kings.

WAY 2: EPIC ENCOUNTERS
Epic encounters are life-defining times in which God reveals Himself and His purpose supernaturally and specifically. Time seems to stop; His voice becomes clear and undeniable. You know you have encountered God. This communication doesn't have to be in an audible voice or even in a vision. It could be a whisper, or a moment when it's undeniable that God is revealing something to you about your purpose.

God appeared to Moses in an epic encounter. What was the reason? God was getting his attention and calling him to go back to Egypt to lead the Israelites out of slavery. Moses had been born in Egypt as a Jew, had grown up in Pharaoh's royal family, and had been privileged to enjoy the highest quality of life. One day, after seeing an Egyptian mistreating a Jewish slave, Moses stepped in and killed the Egyptian. He then fled and lived in Midian for forty years.

At the time of the epic encounter, Moses was eighty years old. God appeared to him, revealing his next season—the next step in his purpose. Moses could not deny God was calling him to this task due to the supernatural way in which God chose to encounter him.

Another example of an epic encounter is Saul's encounter with Jesus on the Damascus road in the book of Acts. Saul was a well-educated religious leader in the community, and responsible for persecuting Christians. Jesus encountered him in a light, spoke to him through an audible voice, and struck him with blindness. I guess Jesus wanted to get his attention. It says in Acts 9:3-6, "As [Paul] neared Damascus on his journey, suddenly a light from heaven flashed around him. He fell to the ground and heard a voice say to him, 'Saul, Saul, why do you persecute me?' 'Who are you, Lord?' Saul asked. 'I am Jesus, whom you are persecuting,' he replied. 'Now get up and go into the city, and you will be told what you must do.'"

Saul encountered the living Jesus. Jesus changed Saul's name to Paul, healed his blindness, and gave him a new purpose. Paul went from persecuting Christians to becoming one of the greatest Christian leaders in history. He wrote two-thirds of the New Testament and traveled all over building the kingdom of God. When you have an epic encounter, it shapes the course of your destiny.

You can have multiple epic encounters in your life. Some may be big; some could be smaller moments in which you knew it was God speaking. These may happen when God is showing you something specific, leading you in a new direction, or doing a deeper work in your personal life. The times I've experienced epic encounters have been those in which God was revealing something specific to me about my life or direction. As I shared previously, one of these moments was the prayer breakfast, when God called me into the ministry. Another was when I had a vision from God that shook me to the bone. I will share about this later in this chapter. Both of these were clear signs and experiences—there was no denying that it was God speaking to me.

WAY 3: TRYING THINGS ON

After college, I held many jobs. Maybe you can relate. My goal was to find what I wanted to do, what I was good at, or what I enjoyed. God took me down a long, winding path that was difficult at times; some of the hardship was self-inflicted. However, it all makes sense now.

In my early postgraduate years, I was a valet parker at a few hotels on Disney property. I waited tables at a friend's restaurant, traded stocks, and sold insurance—all the roles I shared about my story early in the book. Once I was called into the ministry, I started selling life insurance out of the bedroom of my home. It was 100 percent commission-based, which meant it proved to be a total faith walk. Then, for two years, I worked for my mom and stepdad's general contracting company doing public relations and managing customers and job sites.

I didn't know what I was doing. I had no idea that each job I held was preparing me for the future: teaching me to care for people and serve their needs, to live by faith in the area of my finances . . . all of this to make me ready to raise funds for a living and trust that God will supply all my needs, so Karla and I can reach young people. Let's face it: we aren't getting rich giving our lives away to young people who can't pay us back!

Trying things on is one of the main ways God reveals purpose in Scripture and in life. You could say it's like walking through open doors. This concept goes hand-in-hand with the Purpose Cross in how we develop passions and burdens by experiencing them. When we take advantage of the needs and opportunities that present themselves, it is in those places that we do or don't develop a desire for something. Many times, I don't know which direction to go or what decision to make. I find myself praying, "Lord, open the door where *you* want me, and slam shut the doors where you don't." When a door opens, I go through it and try things on.

Trying things on is like being in God's dressing room; it's a place where you get to see how things fit. **Only when you try things on will you know if that outfit on the mannequin looks better on you—or if it even fits. How do you know which clothes fit unless you go try them on?** You can tell pretty quickly how a pair of jeans or shoes fit: too tight, too loose, or just right. My daughter Debi plays soccer, and ever since she was little, we've gone to Academy Sports to buy each new pair of soccer shoes. We haven't bought them on Amazon. Why? Because she's needed to try them on to see how they've fit and how they felt. She's had to take steps in them to see how she's liked them. Then, she's run fast up and down the aisle in them.

It's in the experience and process of trying things on that people find what they enjoy, figure out what they are good at, or develop abilities that will be utilized in the future. The doors we walk through often lead us to other doors and to other seasons, where we learn new skills, develop more character, meet new people, walk through new doors . . . and the cycle continues. You end up closer and closer to the place, purpose, and calling God has for you. It's in the process of trying things on that God begins to reveal the reasons why you are where you are and what you need to learn to be ready for your next season. This is all a part of the experience and how God reveals purpose. Trying things on is a big part of the Purpose Experience. We have to walk down the path of experience in order to grow and find purpose.

Jesus' process in training His disciples demonstrates this principle beautifully. As He prepared His disciples, He gave them an opportunity to see what life with Him was like. He offered them an opportunity to try things on in preparation for His death and resurrection. Later, He would pass them the purpose of taking the gospel into all the world; first, though, they had the opportunity to experience life with Jesus. Peter was the prime example of trying things on. There's an iconic moment in the New Testament when Jesus asks Peter to follow Him—Jesus will make Peter a fisher of men. Most believe that this was the first time Jesus and Peter met—and Jesus asks Peter to lay his life down and follow Him?

What most people don't realize is that this wasn't the first time Jesus met Peter. According to scholars Thomas and Gundry, at the time of this story, Peter had been following Jesus for about a year.[31] Jesus didn't simply walk up and say, "Give up everything and see if you want to be my disciple." Jesus let Peter try things on, get to know Jesus, and see the opportunity for a life greater than what he was living. Peter then said yes to being Jesus' disciple, and walked through the open door, not knowing where it led. As it turned out, the door led to Peter being one of Jesus' inner three friends, and preaching on the day of Pentecost, resulting in three thousand people surrendering to Jesus.

I've found that God continuously reveals His purpose in my life through trying things on. **Many of the greatest purposes of my life were not in my three-, five-, or ten-year business plans.** Coaching a soccer team wasn't something I sought out; it fell into my lap as an opportunity. Saying yes to youth pastoring at two different

---

31   Robert L. Thomas and Stanley N. Gundry. *The NIV Harmony of the Gospels*. (San Francisco: Harper and Row, 1817), 318.

churches resulted in some of the greatest relationships and joys of my life. They were unplanned, as well. These churches were opportunities I felt a peace about trying on. The first one I wanted to say yes to; the second one I didn't want to say yes to but felt that the Lord wanted me to do so. The first church is where God created the foundation that our whole ministry is built upon: identity, freedom, and purpose. The second church held one of my most fruitful seasons of ministry—a time full of raising up young leaders and disciples and sending them out.

One of my mentors, Uncle Jim Peters, always said, "Tim, small doors lead to large rooms!"

One year, Uncle Jim invited me to Germany to help at a U.S. military youth retreat. I said yes to going one time—just to see how I liked it. That trip opened doors to more camps being started around the globe. Traveling the world speaking at U.S. military youth camps was not something I planned. I simply walked through one small, open door with a dozen or so kids to try things on. It led to a massive, worldwide room. Now, speaking at these camps has become one of my favorite things to do.

You won't know how things fit until you try them on! God speaks to you, you learn what you're gifted at, and you find out what brings you frustration or fulfillment. Even when it doesn't work out, it moves you closer to where God wants you to be. God could even be stretching you or teaching you new skills that you'll need later! **Just stay faithful and keep serving where you are right now, until God opens another door.**

Architecture and Graphic Design

Remember the Disney Imagineer—Brian Marschall? His journey of becoming the lead designer at the Magic Kingdom fits right in with this principle of trying things on and walking through open doors. He shared, "I did three years of architecture and hated it. I switched over to graphic design, and I loved it. I thought I wasted three years of my life studying architecture; ironically, I use it every day! It's pretty cool how it worked out. Architecture and graphic design together—that's what I do for environmental design."

In college, Brian started out studying architecture. He got hired at Epcot when he was nineteen. He began drawing on grid paper, thinking of ways to improve things. For example, he brainstormed how to create more space for wheelchair guests in line, solving spatial issues. Then, a few weeks later, his configurations and ideas would come to life. Brian got requests for more of these kinds of things and became known as the guy who can draw. His supervisors took his drawings to the team of Imagineers; one day, Brian asked if he could meet the higher-ups too. They happened to meet in a building near where he worked—a building he'd walked by every day without knowing what happened inside. One of the Imagineers he met was a man named Dave Hoffman—a man he would keep in touch with for a long time. Brian worked on projects for Dave for years; eventually, he got hired full-time onto Disney's team.

Think about it: Brian first learned how to think spatially because of architecture and his first job at Epcot. He walked through open doors at a young age and met key people when he had the opportunity. He had no idea what these meetings would turn into. Some of the things he hated doing would later become key tools in his tool belt for landing his dream job! The skills he learned as an architect help him design unique spaces. Some of the projects he worked on and oversaw were Pirates of the Caribbean in Magic Kingdom, Test Track in Epcot, One Man's Dream in Hollywood Studios, Ratatouille, and Cirque du Soleil.

At the time of this writing, Brian is overseeing the Magic Kingdom 50th Anniversary Celebration coming up. He now uses both architecture and graphic design skills every day. This is a perfect example of the way God leads someone into their practical purpose, even if they don't recognize the process as it's happening. How inspiring is that?

God will use all experiences, all the trying on of things, all walking through the open doors, for His purpose in your life. God even used the thing Brian hated in the beginning—architecture—to work toward his benefit. As we said in a previous chapter, all things work together for the good. The bad experiences, lousy jobs, and tough times we face in life—the things that didn't work out the way we wanted—and even our past mistakes are all part of the experiences God will use to lead us into our purpose. Don't allow these things to paralyze you; instead, allow them to propel you into your purpose!

Proverbs says that the steps of the righteous are ordered by God. **God is a God of movement—not stagnation. We have to keep moving, keep saying yes to Him, and**

walking through new doors. As we continue to "try things on," He will lead us into our purpose for our current season.

WAY 4: SNAPSHOTS

Way before smart phones and digital cameras, you had to hope and pray that your photographs would come out looking good. You never knew until you developed the film. I even remember using disposable cameras: pointing, aiming, snapping a picture. You'd think you got a great shot, only to have it come back blurry, too far away, or with bad lighting. However, when you got a good photo, it felt rewarding.

When a picture was taken before digital cameras, the light entered the camera and an image was created on the film. In order for that image to come to life, it had to be taken into a darkroom and developed with chemicals. Over time, it became visible to the eye. You could then print pictures. God may give you a vision of the big picture He's calling you to; however, sometimes the details haven't yet developed—they're still fuzzy. You don't know exactly how it's going to happen. You only have a glimpse, a direction, to get you moving. You only have enough information to go off of for your current season of life. This is where we must walk in obedience to what God has revealed to us in this moment, until He shows us the next piece of the puzzle.

A snapshot of your purpose could take the form of an actual vision, a dream, a word God gives you, or just a general understanding of the path He wants you to take. Over time, that picture becomes more and more clear. The longer you live and pursue the things set before you, the more clarity you'll gain about His calling for your life.

Genesis 37 tells us the story of Joseph's dream. He saw his brothers, mother, and father all bow down to him. Let's take a look at the details in verses 6-9:

> *"Listen to this dream I had: We were binding sheaves of grain out in the field when suddenly my sheaf rose and stood upright, while your sheaves gathered around mine and bowed down to it." His brothers said to him, "Do you intend to reign over us? Will you actually rule us?" And they hated him all the more because of his dream and what he had said. Then he had another dream, and he told it to his brothers. "Listen," he said, "I*

had another dream, and this time the sun and moon and eleven stars were bowing down to me."

Joseph didn't know what this all meant, or how this was going to happen; he just knew God was going to elevate him in a big way. He didn't know it would result in him rising to be second-in-command over all of Egypt during a time of famine; he didn't know that all of Israel would be spared because of his strategy to save food. God didn't show him the whole process up front; instead, He led Joseph on a journey. God just gave him a snapshot of the big picture of what He was, generally, going to do. If God had shown him everything up front, Joseph probably would have been scared and said no to it!

The process God took Joseph through was difficult, filled with ups and downs. He was sold into slavery by his brothers, became Potiphar's servant, was falsely accused of sexually assaulting Potiphar's wife, was thrown into prison, interpreted dreams while there, and was put in charge of prisoners. Finally, Joseph interpreted Pharaoh's dream when nobody else could. In one day, he went from the pit of prison to the palace, and became the second-in-command of all Egypt. God had to take him through a dark process, develop him, and prepare him to contain the vision God had burned into his heart.

THE VISION THAT SHOOK ME

A few years after God called me into youth ministry, I was struggling because I wasn't sure where God was taking me—what the future held. One night, a friend and I spent hours in prayer while our wives were away at a weekend retreat. During this time, the Lord gave me a vision. I'd never had one before, so I didn't understand what was happening, other than that God was revealing deep secrets and long-term vision for my life in ministry.

I saw two giant mountaintops, flat and separated by a big, bottomless chasm filled with fire. Young people were walking off the cliffs into the fire. One by one, by the thousands, these kids were falling to their destruction. The side of the cliff that the kids were on was brown, hard, dusty ground. Coming from that side, I could feel a depth of despair—a sense of death—a lack of hope and life. On the other side of the cliff was a beautiful, lush, green pasture with three thrones. On the middle throne was God; on the left was Jesus. This was a place full of life, peace, and tranquility. I knew it represented heaven.

In the vision, I began to weep uncontrollably as my gaze fixed on the brown side of the chasm. Along with the kids falling off the cliff, I also saw kids by the thousands sitting and kneeling on the ground in bondage. Some were tied up with ropes to pieces of wood or to trees; others sat in chains, linked to small, three-foot posts.

Jesus led me around this area to see the magnitude of the situation. Isolation and hopelessness were the dominant feelings. Then, Jesus handed me keys and giant shearers. The keys were like the big ones you see in movies, used to unlock prisoners. The giant shearers looked like what you use to trim bushes. I began walking around, cutting ropes and unlocking young people from chains. I'd look into their eyes and say, "Go! Be free!" I began running as fast as I could to the next kid and the next, each time cutting ropes and unlocking chains. One by one, they began to walk towards the edge of the cliff. When they got there, a long, clear, glass-like walkway appeared from one side to the other. At first, the walkway was narrow; in single file, the kids walked across, looking down at the fire below as they approached the other side.

Then things got *really* intense. I felt an urgency rise up inside of me to set as many free as I could. As far as the eye could see, massive numbers of young people sat in bondage. I couldn't get to all of them, but the Lord just said, "Tim, just speak the word." I began pointing to groups of kids all over who were tied up or in chains, and yelling, "GO! BE FREE!" By the thousands, kids broke free, sprinted to the edge of the cliff, and crossed to safety on the other side.

It was so vivid. I could feel the fire. I could smell the dust. I could hear the cries of the young people. It was as real to me as my computer in front of me right now. This vision shook me to my core. I had to do something, but I didn't know where to begin—or even how this would play out in my life. God gave me a snapshot of the big picture He was calling me to . . . the details would follow later.

The reason God reveals purpose this way is because, like Joseph, He knows how much you can handle. If God had shown me everything I would have to walk through, or the responsibility of what He was entrusting to me, I may not have said yes. Many times, God works this way because, if He showed you the full picture right away, it would scare you. **God doesn't want to overwhelm you, but rather to provoke you to take the first step.**

Many times, snapshots take on the form of a vision, prophetic word, or a picture that God gives you. You only see the general direction, but you don't know how to get there—or even the magnitude of what He is up to. It's simply a snapshot intended to get you moving.

GOD'S DARKROOM

I didn't have a clue how any of what I saw would come to pass. How would we reach thousands of kids? Where would they come from? It took several years to even begin to understand some of the details. It was a long, sometimes dark, road to travel. Gradually, more light was shed upon this purpose as I tried things on, obeyed, and walked through open doors. God is now reaching young people all over the world, and we are raising up leaders who are impacting tens of thousands of their peers.

When God gives you a snapshot, it requires going into the darkroom to develop the vision. Don't despise the darkroom! Through this process, it may feel like God has left you hanging or has abandoned you. God has brought you there *not* to destroy you but to *develop* you! He allowed me to walk through dark and difficult times because that's where character is developed. He had to trust me with the call on my life; He wants to trust *you* with what He's calling you to do. This will require your being developed and made ready for your purpose.

Don't forget in the dark what He showed you in the light! Stop complaining about the dark seasons. God will bring the full picture to pass in due season if you don't quit. Many times, when God reveals His purpose this way, it involves a long period of time—or a lifetime—discovering the details and magnitude of your calling. This is why we must enjoy the process and not simply be obsessed with reaching the destination.

While my vision is not fully developed, the picture has become clearer to me over the years. This book, the study guide, and video series are all a part of the larger-scale vision of seeing massive numbers of young people, young adults, and people of all ages GO, AND BE FREE—just like in my vision!

INTERTWINING PURPOSE

God is not limited to just one way of revealing purpose. I'm sure that, as you read this chapter, you can think of other ways God has revealed purpose in Scripture, or ways in which He has coached you into your purpose. Many times, He will lead us by combining and intertwining these principles together. My vision involved an epic encounter and a snapshot, initially. Then, as I've walked it out over the past nineteen years, God has used trying things on as a part of the revelation. **All in all, it's not primarily about the vision but about following the leading of the Vision-Giver.**

God may not show you a vision; He may give you one word, or an impression of what direction to go in. He may whisper to you to solve a problem in the world—to become a doctor, business owner, teacher, missionary, or artist. You may not know what it'll look like, or how it will come to pass, but He gives you a snapshot of what He wants you to do next. Then, as you take steps and walk through adversity, the picture becomes clearer.

Maybe God has given you a vision, but you feel discouraged that it hasn't come to pass yet. Maybe you're wondering where God is. Others may be praying right now that God would show you His vision for your life. In any case, don't give up. God will come through. He will show you in due season. As we close this chapter, let me leave you with a few thoughts.

The Bible says, **"Do not despise these small beginnings, for the LORD rejoices to see the work begin"** (Zechariah 4:10, ESV). Zechariah 4:6 reminds us that it is "'**Not by might, nor by power, but by my Spirit,' says the LORD Almighty.**" We need to be willing to start somewhere. Start small, and watch God be faithful to promote you and breathe upon what you are doing!

Your purpose may involve stewarding another man's gift or company before God gives you your own. Luke 16:12 (NKJV) says, "If you have not been faithful in what is another man's, who will give you what is your own?" Be faithful with what you've been given so far—no matter how hard it is. God will show you the next steps when you are ready.

God wants to speak to you. He wants to coach you into your purpose. As you go through the process, I pray that you'll begin to recognize the ways God has been speaking to you and revealing His purpose to you all along. May you discover the reasons you were born. May you have epic encounters. May you continue to try things on and walk through the open doors God has placed in your life. May God plant a vision in your heart and show you a snapshot of what He is calling you to do! This is what experiencing purpose is all about.

QUESTIONS FOR SELF-REFLECTION

Which of the ways God speaks have you experienced most frequently? Can you recall a specific instance in which you sensed Him in this way?

_____

_____

_____

_____

Which of the four coaching methods do you think your life most closely aligns with, and why?

_____

_____

_____

_____

How does the analogy of a spiritual "darkroom" change your perspective on what the process of fulfilling your purpose may look like?

_____

_____

_____

_____

How do you think our culture and the values we hold contribute to a sense of impatience when it comes to discovering purpose and developing as people? What does God's Word have to say about this (find a few verses or scripture passages)?

_____

_____

_____

_____

CHAPTER 8

DARE TO DREAM DIFFERENTLY!

As Karla and I walked out of the *One Man's Dream* attraction at Disney's Hollywood Studios, something in my heart clicked! I was mesmerized by what I'd just experienced. I stood speechless, in deep thought, for several minutes as I stared at one picture that brought everything into perspective for me. This finally explained why I'd been so enamored with Walt Disney all these years.

You see, during my wilderness days as a Disney hotel valet, I'd often receive free park tickets from guests and would go after work. I always thought the lure was due to the fun—I got to be a big kid. However, when Karla and I began dating and launched our ministry, People of Purpose, I sensed an even stronger feeling of appreciation and love for Disney inside of myself.

It was on the day that we walked through this attraction that I finally pinpointed the cause. *One Man's Dream* is an interactive gallery that displays memorabilia from all the Disney time periods. It has projects, pictures, props, and authentic artifacts that tell the Disney story over a number of decades. As we walked through this hallway of heroism and read every sign, something deep in my soul was stirred and drawn in—I experienced a sense of child-like amazement.

At the end of the exhibit, we watched a fifteen-minute documentary about Walt Disney. It led to my light-bulb moment. The video shared information about his family, his struggles, the early journey of his vision to become an artist, and the process by which the movies and parks had been created. I was fascinated by this short black-and-white film that held behind-the-scenes stories. It gripped me. But *why*? What was the deeper meaning? When we walked out of the show and into the merchandise shop, my eyes were drawn to that all-important photograph I first mentioned. It's a picture of Walt standing on dirt, in front of a silhouette of Cinderella's castle, the iconic image of the Magic Kingdom. On the bottom of the picture was one word: *VISION!*

The word struck a chord deep inside my soul. It was like something dormant was suddenly awakened! *That's why I've been fascinated with Walt Disney World.* It spoke to my spirit about how one man's dream changed the world! Walt Disney saw things in his mind before they ever came to be. He had a big vision—a vision different from everyone else's—that has impacted hundreds of millions of people around the world. God spoke to me through this example about my purpose, and the importance of chasing after God's dreams for my life. With each Disney encounter, God was subtly inspiring me to not give up. He had been preparing me for this moment for years, even though I couldn't see it yet.

God has put a vision inside of you as well, even if you can't see it yet! He sees things in you that you don't yet see yourself. Maybe you're like I was, and you don't yet have a vision for your life. Or possibly, you have a vision, but God wants to take the limitations off of your perspective so you can dream bigger and differently than ever before. No matter where you are right now, recognize that God wants to give you His vision for your life. He believes in you, and He wants to show you what He sees. Keep in mind that your calling may look different than what you originally thought it would be. It will change and grow over time.

So far, we've talked about how your purpose involves a problem you were created to solve, how you need to find your identity in order to walk in freedom, how God wants you to become possessed with purpose by experiencing His presence, the different crossroads on the Purpose Cross, and the ways God coaches you into your purpose. We've nailed down a lot of specifics. Now, I want to bring it all in together by talking about how dreaming differently—having a vision—is key to living out your purpose.

WHAT IS A VISION?

About two years before saying yes to youth ministry, a friend of my dad's asked me a really deep but simple question that had a profound impact on my life. One day, after church, He asked me, "Tim, if you could do anything in the world, and you could not fail, and money wasn't an obstacle, what would you do? What would you attempt for God?"

I thought for a minute, and gave the only answer that made any sense, even though I didn't actually believe there was any way to actually obtain this. I said, "I would use soccer and surfing to share the gospel around the world." That question has never left me, and I've asked thousands of kids the same thing. What this man was asking was this: "What is your life's vision?" Little did I know that my simple answer would become reality—that these two passions would be used every year as a part of the plan to lead young people to Christ and disciple them!

What is vision? How do we get it, and where does it come from? Vision is defined as the act or power of seeing or imagining something. **Vision is the big picture in your mind of what you want to accomplish.** It's the ability to imagine and visualize a desired outcome. It's seeing the end result, outcome, or impact of something you want to do. Once you have vision, you can work toward a goal.

On October 1, 1971, five years after the great Walt Disney passed away, Disney World held its grand opening for the Magic Kingdom. During the dedication ceremony, one of the executives turned to Mrs. Disney and said, "Isn't it a shame that Walt didn't live to see this?"

Mrs. Disney replied, "He did see it—that's why it's here!"

Wow. What a statement. This is what vision is all about. This is why that famous picture of Disney is so powerful. It paints a picture of the power of vision! Walt saw the Magic Kingdom in his mind long before it was ever built. Vision can begin with something simple and grow into something much larger. Even with the enormity of what Disney has become, the founder's vision began with something simple. Walt said, "I only hope that we never lose sight of one thing . . . that it was all started with a mouse." Everything we see today began with the idea of Mickey Mouse. Through these small beginnings, Disney reinvented and revolutionized family entertainment. God's Word says, "Despise not small beginnings." Begin small, and watch God give you more. Your vision may be tiny, or even non-existent, right now, but as you take steps of obedience, it will grow. **Being faithful to your practical purpose now will allow you to step into your future vision later.**

The purpose of your initial vision helps to influence and fund your bigger vision. In *One Man's Dream*, Walt Disney stated, "Mickey was simply a little personality assigned to the purposes of laughter. He brought in the money, which saved the day and he enabled us to explore our medium, and paved the way for our more elaborate screen ventures!"[32] Basically, without the original vision of Mickey, the funding for the larger vision would never have been available. Walt moved in faith with the small vision of Mickey Mouse (originally named Mortimer Mouse), and it paved the way for vision expansion. When you begin to live out your vision where you are right now, God will provide for your needs and continue to expand it.

WALT'S VISION

"Disneyland: it all started from a daddy with two daughters wondering where he could take them where he could have a little fun with them too."[33]

> *"We believed in our idea—a family park where parents and children could have fun—together."*
>
> —Walt Disney

Walt Disney had vision like few others. When he formally dedicated Disneyland on its opening day, July 17, 1955, he closed his speech by saying this: ". . . with the hope that it will be a source of joy and inspiration to all the world." This was a big-picture vision. The method by which its details came together over decades is now visible to the entire world.

---

32 Phil May, Ken Welch, Ian Fraser, and Chris Boardman Billy Byers. "Walt Disney: One Man's Dream." USA, 1981.

33 Ibid.

I believe Walt's greater purpose on this earth was to bring families together, so they could laugh, play, and make memories. Having quality time together, making memories, and connecting has never been more important than it is today. Walt's vision helped families do just that. His bigger vision is what brought a practical solution to a problem on earth.

Vision involves seeing what others don't. Walt saw what others didn't, and it had a huge impact on the world, the movie industry, animation, and theme parks. Almost every child growing up in the modern world is impacted by the life of Walt Disney. It was the clarity of Walt's bigger vision that gave him the power to live out his practical purpose. We must get a vision for our lives so that we can fulfill the spiritual and practical purposes God has for us.

Walt Disney says, "A good ending is vital to a picture, the single most important element, because it is what the audience takes with them out of the theater." We stated earlier that vision is about the big-picture ending. So I ask you this: What does the movie of your life look like? When your life comes to a close, what do you want those in the audience to walk away with? What do you want to be known for? What do you want your life's legacy to be? We see clearly the impact of Walt's life and vision. What about yours?

FINDING A BIBLICAL VISION

"Without inspiration, we would perish."

—Walt Disney

True vision comes from God and leads to purposeful living. Without a vision, we walk around lost—just surviving instead of thriving. We lose hope and slowly drift away from God. However, when we get a vision, we begin to live the abundant life for which God created us.

Proverbs 29:18 (KJV) says, "Where there is no vision the people perish, but he that keepeth the law, happy is he." This is one of my favorite Bible verses because it carries powerful truths. Take a look at how the different translations capture it:

- Amplified Bible: "Where there is no vision [no revelation of God and his word], the people are unrestrained; But happy *and* blessed is he who keeps the law [of God]."
- New Living Translation: "When people do not accept divine guidance, they run wild. But whoever obeys the law is joyful."
- God's Word Translation: "Without prophetic vision people run wild, but blessed are those who follow God's teachings."
- Geneva Bible: "Where there is no vision, the people decay: but he that keepeth the law is blessed."
- King James Version: "Where there is no vision, the people perish; but he that keepeth the law, happy is he."

Without vision, people die inside. They lack purpose. This leads to boredom, and boredom is the breeding ground for an idle mind. Scripture says that an idle mind is the devil's playground. Proverbs 29:18 shows that having no vision will cause a generation to run wild, be unrestrained, lack self-control, and decay. This is clearly happening in today's society, as so many are unbridled and affected by issues like those we've already explored.

Most of the time this scripture is shared, pastors and preachers tend to focus on the negative aspect of it: People are perishing without vision. However, I believe it's a two-sided coin. There is a converse truth: Where there is vision, people will live!

Your life's vision can only come from God. The word "vision" in Proverbs 29:18 is the Hebrew word *châzôwn*. It refers to a *divine* vision, dream, or revelation. God must reveal what He wants us to do, or we will run wild and perish!

God's vision brings direction to your life and produces benefits you cannot buy. The Amplified Bible translation likens the vision in this verse to a revelation of God and His Word. Other versions use phrases such as "prophetic vision" and "divine guidance." Others say that vision produces joy and happiness. The bottom line is that all vision and revelation come from God. If you're lacking vision, spend time in His Word. Ask Him for it. He will show you.

Vision will put you on God's path of purpose instead of the world's. Most of the time, we tell young people to stop sinning—to stop partying and start going to church. While these may be desired goals, this approach is merely behavior modification. It won't work. What they need is a glimpse of God's vision for their lives to keep them from going down those alternative paths. Once they acquire vision, they'll begin to say, "I don't want to go out and party. I don't want to sleep around, do drugs, look at pornography. I see where God is taking me, and I want His vision for my life." Our behaviors lose their control over our lives as we choose to pursue His vision instead of the world's. When you get a glimpse of God's perspective, you'll begin to live with purpose!

THE POWER OF PERSPECTIVE

True vision is having God's perspective about our lives and the world in which we live. To get clarity about His vision, His point of view, we must get His perspective—we must come higher and get closer to Him to see what He sees. Isaiah 55:9 says, "As the heavens are higher than the earth, so are my ways higher than your ways and my thoughts higher than your thoughts." Seeing things God's way will help us see beyond the obstacles and challenges, the excuses and fears, beyond all the unknowns and uncertainties.

Hope in the Lord gives you true, biblical vision. Hope is illustrated through the picture of an eagle in Isaiah 40:31: "But those who hope in the LORD will renew their strength. They will soar on wings like eagles; they will run and not grow weary, they will walk and not be faint." You can soar when you have hope in the Lord and see things from His perspective. Perspective provides power. The eagle's wings are designed to catch the wind, so it can soar without even flapping them. They can do this for miles at a time. Just as the eagle has this ability to fly in the winds of adversity, hope allows us to rest and soar, knowing that God is in control.

Eagles also have incredible vision. Their eyesight is about 4-8 times better than that of humans. They can even see a rabbit from up to two miles away![34] If we had their vision, we could see an ant crawling on the ground from the roof of a ten-story building, or make out the expressions on basketball players' faces from the highest seats in the arena. Eagles have a 340-degree visual field (compared to humans' 180-degree visual field). They see colors more vividly than we do, and they can even see the UV light in the urine trails of some of their prey.[35]

---

34 "The Best Eyes in the Animal Kingdom." *All About Eyes*, https://allabouteyes.com/best-eyes-animal-kingdom/.

35 Natalie Wolchover. "What If Humans Had Eagle Vision?" *Live Science*, https://www.livescience.com/18658-humans-eagle-vision.html.

An eagle's survival is based on its vision. If it cannot see clearly, it can't hunt and fulfill its purpose in the food chain. If we do not have clear vision, we cannot fulfill *our* God-given purpose, either.

Many times, life beats us down and we lose hope, which leads to a lack of vision. The storms bring doubt, fear, and disappointment. We wonder why God is allowing this to happen. Unless we go higher in our perspective, we won't be able to see the purpose in it all. Hope in God gives you panoramic vision—a vision that's colorful, clear, and beyond your natural ability. Our victory as Christians lies in us getting God's perspective. Once we do that, we can see into the vision and the future that He has for us.

YOUR SIGNIFICANCE IS HIDDEN IN YOUR DIFFERENCE

Find your difference, and you will find your purpose. A key to finding purpose is discovering the vision you're passionate about and fulfilling it differently than anyone else. While Walt Disney had a big vision, there was something about his vision that separated him from all the others. What he did was unique from what others had done or attempted. Even his own wife questioned him about his vision. Walt shared, "When I started on Disneyland, my wife used to say, 'But why do you want to build an amusement park? They're so dirty.' I told her that was just the point: Mine wouldn't be." Walt's significance was hidden in his vision of building an amusement park *differently* than anybody else ever had!

Daring to dream differently requires asking yourself some key questions: What do you do that's unique? If I were to line up ten thousand people who do what you do (or want to do), what would make you different? How do you sing, draw, think, help others, or lead in your own special way? How do your talents stick out from the crowd?

When you find that, you'll discover the very reason God has created you! As Rick Warren says in *The Purpose-Driven Life,* "God designed each of us so there would be no duplication in the world. No one has the exact same mix of factors that make you unique. That means no one else on earth will ever be able to play the role God planned for you."[36]

---

36 Rick Warren. *The Purpose-Driven Life: What on Earth Am I Here For?* Zondervan, 2002.

I'm pretty sure no other soccer coach does what I do the way I do it. I take my team on mission trips (including taking individual players on U.S. military ministry trips), bring my team on leadership retreats to North Carolina, have group Bible studies and counseling times, ask them the tough questions about masturbation and pornography, and take the seniors on a purpose training retreat to go through this very curriculum you are reading today. This is what makes me different. It's the reason my life has the significance and impact that it does. This is just one area of my purpose and how I fulfill my calling differently than everyone else.

Being different is a gift, not a curse. Many young people get made fun of, feel insecure, or believe that people don't get them because they're different. Have you ever felt that way? Remember that God made you the way you are so that you can stand out and be unique, not blend in and be average. People *without* vision try to be like everyone else. Don't pick a college, career path, or other path just because somebody else does! Go down your own path—the path God made for you! Don't let your life be a "repost" of anyone else's; allow your unique calling and purpose to be on display every day.

In order to get a vision, you must discover your significance through your difference. This is what daring to dream differently is all about. God gives us the ability to see what others don't. Start dreaming big, start dreaming differently, and change the world!

Here's another important point about your difference: **Being different requires being authentic.** God's anointing flows through your authenticity! Don't try to be just like someone else; don't succumb to the pressure to be bigger than anyone else. Be the best version of you that you can be. Be the best you God created! The anointing—His power on your life's vision—comes through being authentic.

Once I began speaking all over the world, I noticed that there were unspoken expectations on me when I came to minister. People began hearing about how God moved in the services, especially through miracles. I remember one time, when I was preaching on a TV station, my friend who'd invited me made a statement to the audience before we started filming: "Get ready. God is going to speak through Tim and give you a word and prophesy over your life."

I remember going to the back of the room and getting on my knees. "Lord, I am going to be Tim, your son—nothing more or less. The results are up to you. I just am going to be the best Tim Waisanen God created. If people get healed and you speak to me about their lives, then you get the glory. If not, then I will just speak what you tell me. Unless you speak, God, I've got nothing!"

So many people minimize what God is calling them to do based on what it looks like in the natural: the opportunity, the numbers, the size—how many people they're influencing. They discount their purpose and dwarf their calling because they don't feel that it's significant. Your effectiveness is *not* based solely on numbers. If God has called you to do something, then it is significant!

I'll never forget what Mike Coleman, a mentor of mine, said one day: "Tim, I am not a good dad based upon the quantity of kids I have, but on the quality of kids I raise!" Having more kids doesn't make me a better dad, but spending better time with them does. That's always stuck with me. You may not be impacting thousands of people, but to that one person you *are* reaching, you mean everything. Impact as many as you can, but remember that it's not about the quantity of people or the size of the vision. It's about the quality of the impact and the transformation that takes place as a result.

Now that we've laid a foundation for vision and its importance, I want to show you two simple steps you can take to discover your vision: narrowing your focus and making those strengths better.

STEP 1: NARROW YOUR FOCUS

What is your brand? What do you want to be known for? Most people are known for *one main thing* they did on this earth. When I say Michael Jordan, Paul McCartney, George Lucas, Jennifer Lopez, Steve Jobs, Martin Luther King, Jr., Billy Graham, or Tiger Woods, what comes to mind? Usually, there is one main thing they're known for.

Your experiences help fine-tune your vision story and purpose statement. If this hasn't happened yet, just wait—it will. When you begin to live with purpose, your experiences will help you discover what's different about you. You'll be able to narrow your focus—gain clarity on what you really want to do and how.

When I started out in youth ministry, I was a generalist. I did *all* things youth ministry: the fun and crazy games, retreats and camps, youth services, invite nights, preaching, relationship building, mission trips. For the first fifteen years, I experienced what worked and what didn't, what areas I felt called to, and what I was best at. This process helped me gain clarity about my unique contributions and differences, so that I could narrow my focus. I now focus my life primarily on what I'm best at: preaching, counseling, and purpose training.

In 1963, Martin Luther King, Jr., gave his famous "I Have a Dream" speech. Over two hundred thousand people showed up. His whole life experience had led him to this moment. I wonder how long it took him to arrive at this vision? How much adversity did he have to go through? What experiences did he have? How many years of injustice did he witness to shape this vision and make this speech? King led a rally in Washington, DC, in 1957, which attracted twenty-five thousand; ultimately, this had little impact due to the lack of energy around the Civil Rights movement at that time. In 1958, he was stabbed at one of his book signings. Instead of quitting, King was relentless; he worked for six more years to build the momentum that led up to his famous "I Have A Dream" speech. Everything in his life led to that moment. The march led to the passing of both the Civil Rights Act of 1964 and the Voting Rights Act of 1965.[37]

Everything in your life will eventually lead to you narrowing your focus. It may take years, but now you're aware of what you can look for—you can be at peace, even though you don't have it all figured out yet. After all, who does?

Here's another important point: **Narrowing your focus makes it easier to say no!** Once you narrow your focus, your yes becomes so important that it's easy to turn down opportunities that don't align with your vision. In Greg McKeown's book, *Essentialism: The Disciplined Pursuit of Less,* the author's main value proposition is this: "Only once you give yourself permission to stop trying to do it all, stop saying yes to everyone, can you make your highest contribution to the things that really matter."[38] God will put a vision in your heart that will require saying no to more things. Learn to say no so that you can say yes to what you're most effective at doing!

---

37 "March on Washington for Jobs and Freedom." *Kinginstitute.stanford,* https://kinginstitute.stanford.edu/encyclopedia/march-washington-jobs-and-freedom ; "Prayer Pilgrimage for Freedom." Kinginstitute.stanford.edu. May 17, 1957. https://kinginstitute.stanford.edu/encyclopedia/prayer-pilgrimage-freedom.

38 Greg McKeown. *Essentialism: The Disciplined Pursuit of Less.* Currency Publishing, 2014. 4.

Over my years in youth ministry, I narrowed my focus and discovered my "dream." I have a dream that every teenager and young adult can discover the abundant life Jesus promises in His Word! I want to spend the rest of my life helping young people find their identity, freedom, and purpose through Christ. My and my wife's ultimate big-picture vision is to "awaken purpose within young leaders to influence every area of culture with the gospel." That's what I'm best at, and all I want to do. I've seen many young people fall away from their faith because they haven't addressed and resolved key issues in their lives. I've seen so much doubt about who God is. I want young people to experience the real Jesus. It was my key experiences that caused me to realize the "brand" of my life: to be known as the best youth speaker, counselor, and purpose trainer on the planet. When people think of needing someone to speak at their young adult event, to counsel their teen, or to help young adults find God's purpose and get unstuck, I want my name on the top of that list. I want my life to reflect the glory of God in this way.

What do *you* want to be known for? What does God want the brand of *your* life to be?

STEP 2: FIND YOUR GIFT AND MAKE IT BETTER

Narrowing our focus will allow us to utilize our strengths for maximum impact. When we focus on making our strengths better, our gifts will open doors we never even imagined! The experiences I had enabled me to discover my strengths, producing a clearer vision that led, ultimately, to this book and curriculum. My focus on bettering my gift has opened doors around the world I could never have dreamed would open for me.

Focusing on strength is the foundation of the Disney Principle. Disney takes a good idea and dreams up ways to make it even better. When Disney Imagineers develop an idea, they'll ask questions such as, "How is this different than what anybody else has built? What can we do to make it better?" Utilizing their strengths, they consider how they can improve and take their offerings to the next level.

You are a gift to the world. What you do with your life is your gift back to God! When you get a vision and focus on your gifts, doors will open and you will become a blessing to those around you. According to John Maxwell, one of the world's greatest authorities on leadership, we should focus on our strengths to maximize our effectiveness as leaders. If you're naturally gifted—let's say a seven out of ten—you can become a ten with some work. However, if you are naturally a three at something, you might raise your skill level to a seven, but you'll probably never become a ten in that area.

Consider this statement as it relates to your life:

When I am doing _____, heaven comes to earth and has an impact on others.

What are you good at, and how can you become even better at it? What skills of yours have had a positive impact on others? Proverbs 18:16 (author's paraphrase) says, "A man's gift will make room for him and will bring him in front of prominent men." Walt Disney's gift brought him in front of the wealthiest, most powerful, and most famous people alive. We don't have to make room for our gifts; our gifts will make room for us. They will open doors so that we can fulfill the vision of God. Once you find your difference, clarify your vision, and narrow your focus, you can maximize your strengths and live out your purpose. Remember, purpose is a process. This process includes getting a vision for your life, dreaming differently, and becoming the best at your dream that you can be.

Is your heart good soil, ready for God to plant His vision into it? If soil is dry, or lacks nutrients, seeds cannot grow. Get your heart to a place where it's ready and willing to receive God's vision! This is why we focused so much on the spiritual side of purpose in the early chapters: to get your heart ready to receive!

God chose you to be born at this time in history. He created you with specific talents, abilities, and gifts. He has a vision for you to fulfill. Maybe you're struggling with finding it; maybe you have some idea of what it looks like but are afraid to step out in faith. Either way, let me encourage you with Joel 2:28 and Acts 2:17, which say, "In the last days, God says, 'I will pour out my Spirit on all people. Your sons and daughters will prophesy, your young men will see visions, your old men will dream dreams.'" Joel 2:28 uses the Hebrew word *chizzâyôwn* for vision, which means "expectation by dream." When we are in His presence, He will pour out His Spirit and put His dreams into our hearts. Get your heart ready, and ask with expectation for Him to reveal His vision for your life!

I wanted to conclude this chapter with a quote that Brian, the Disney Imagineer, shared at the end of our lunch together. When Brian finished his story, he made this statement: "That's what I am here for! I'm not here for the easy road; I'm here to wrestle with something, to figure it out, and to run into the wall. **I'm here to fail and fail until I actually succeed.** It's problem-solving—that's what I do. I have to embrace that. It's nice to try to solve something that is new and fresh and unknown, that has never been done before." Walt Disney's vision was so big that it is still impacting the world today. It was so different and clear that it's still changing the life of a man like Brian, who is carrying out that dream fifty years after Magic Kingdom opened.

Walt started with a mouse. The first night I ever had a youth service, it was just me and one kid playing basketball. Dream big, but begin small. God is calling you to dream differently and solve a problem. Our vision should be big enough that it impacts others after we are gone. Narrow your focus, use your strengths, and do it in a unique way. Be willing to step out in faith. Risk comparisons, risk failure, risk the I-told-you-so accusations, risk security, risk provision. Take a chance on God. Dream differently. Dream big. Take a step, and watch God fulfill His vision for your life.

When you close your eyes, what do you see? What are you doing? Who are you doing it with? Who are you doing it for, and what is the impact you have? Can you see it, like a movie preview? At the end of your life, what will people say about you? What will they thank you for the most? What prayers to God will your life answer? What are you doing that causes heaven to come down to earth?

QUESTIONS FOR SELF-REFLECTION

If everyone got paid the same hourly wage, no matter what job they did, what would you want to do?

_____

_____

_____

_____

_____

What is it that you do differently than anyone else? How do you do it uniquely?

_____

_____

_____

_____

_____

What are some things you see God is currently blessing and wanting to do in the earth right now?

_____

_____

_____

_____

_____

How do your passions and dreams align with God's current work, from what you can see around you? In other words, where does your passion align with the needs God is meeting in your world?

_____

_____

_____

_____

CHAPTER 9

GOD'S GUIDELINES FOR YOUR PURPOSE STATEMENT

"Dreams, ideas, and plans not only are an escape, they give me purpose, a reason to hang on."

—Walt Disney

When we take God's visions and dreams for our lives and create a practical plan, they will produce purpose. Purpose brings hope! Hope is what gives you a reason to hang on.

It gives you something to focus on—the good things, the possibilities of what God created you for—instead of focusing on the negatives and problems all around you. You focus on what you can do and not on what you can't do. You see opportunities, not obstacles. The result is hope! This concept is what purpose is all about.

Your focus will either feed your faith or feed your fears. You choose: do you want faith or fear of failure? This is what this book is all about: inspiring faith and hope in this next generation that God is good, and His plans are good. When we experience Jesus and begin to move in faith by writing things down, creating a plan, and being intentional, it is actually an act of faith! Our faith becomes visible, tangible, practical, and it causes us to come alive with hope and purpose! This next section is all about putting hope on paper.

From the very beginning, God has given us the guidance we need. He's shown us clearly the things He wants us to notice—even to the point of creating things in the sky and writing them clearly in His Word. When we pay attention to these principles, it provides big-picture instructions for stepping into our purpose.

Genesis chapter 1 says that God created the sun, moon, and stars in the sky to rule over the day and night, but also to separate light from darkness. God declared that these would be indicators of signs and seasons marked by Him. From the foundation of creation, God was giving us guidelines that made days, nights, and years clear.

The book of Matthew talks about how three wise men followed a star to Bethlehem. They were well-learned men who had studied the sciences—astronomy, as well as biblical prophecy. When they saw the Star of David, they knew something major was happening—that a king was being born. The kings knew there was something special about this king because of the position of the star. It was the sign that Jesus had been born. Scholars say it took the men about two years to actually arrive at Jesus' doorstep. It was this Star of David that acted as their guiding force to help them locate the Messiah.

Stars represent the big-picture principles that guide you to your purpose. Just like the wise men were guided by and followed the Star of David, we also need something to guide us.

God created stars to separate night from day and to indicate times and seasons. They are a guiding force in our everyday lives. In the same way, God has some spiritual stars to follow. In this chapter, we'll look at what should become your Star of David: your compass that points you "North" to your purpose. We'll begin to pull together everything we've talked about in order to create your vision story and purpose statement. These statements will allow you to practically apply your spiritual purpose; they will include your personal identity and how God has wired you. They will become your guiding stars for years to come!

A vision story is a broad, general description of what you see yourself doing. It's that movie trailer we discussed in the last chapter. Everyone has different opinions of what a vision story/statement looks like—how long it should be, what it should include, and so on. For our purposes, your vision story can be anywhere from a few paragraphs to two pages. Mine is about a page-and-a-half.

Your purpose statement is a more concise, boiled-down theme derived from your vision story. It will act as your guiding North Star. When life gets uncertain or unclear, or when important decisions need to be made, you can look to these guiding statements to stay on course.

You may be able to take the concepts we've discussed so far and articulate your vision story and purpose statement at the end of this chapter. However, you may need further direction. We have a study guide and video series that will walk you through this entire process. More about these resources later. For now, here are some basic things to consider about these two "guiding stars" and how they can remind us of our path when life gets dark.

GOD'S FIRST GUIDELINE: THE GREAT COMMANDMENT

Loving God and others will lead you to your purpose. In order to write our statements, we must first look at God's priorities. We unpacked these in the "Crossroads of Purpose" chapter. God's first priority on earth for us is twofold: to love Him and love others. The Great Commandment of Mark 12:30-31 (NKJV) says, "'And you shall love the Lord your God with all your heart, with all your soul, with all your mind, and with all your strength.' This is the first commandment. And the second, like it, is this: 'You shall love your neighbor as yourself.' There is no other commandment greater than these."

We must first love God with everything in us. Then, we must love our neighbors. The problem is that many *don't* love their neighbors precisely because they don't love themselves. Just look at our world today. In Colossians 3, God describes forgiveness and love as "your basic, all-purpose garment" (the Message translation). The Word admonishes us to never be without it. Loving God enables you to love yourself, and loving yourself empowers you to love your neighbor. If you're unable to love others, it's likely because one of the two prerequisites is missing.

GOD'S SECOND GUIDELINE: THE GREAT COMMISSION

God's second priority for us on earth is the Great Commission. In Matthew 28:18-20, Jesus said to His disciples, "All authority in heaven and on earth has been given to me. Therefore go and make disciples of all nations, baptizing them in the name of the Father and of the Son and of the Holy Spirit, and teaching them to obey everything I have commanded you. And surely I am with you always, to the very end of the age."

Everything we put energy into should somehow impact others by showing them the love of God. This is the purpose and mission of the church. It's our personal mandate as well. No matter what purpose we live out, at the core, we are to make disciples.

HOW THE GUIDELINES COME TOGETHER

One day, I asked my friend, Rabbi Gary Fernandez—a Christian and one of the wisest men I know—what biblical purpose looks like. What he said struck me, and it's become a key focus in the way that I help others find purpose. He said, "Tim, true biblical purpose is wrapped around the one Hebraic concept of *chesed*."

Of course, I was like, "Uh, what is that?"

Gary shared that *chesed* is Hebrew for "acts of loving kindness." Biblical purpose is simply having a relationship with Jesus so that He can begin leading you to bless others. The most important thing in blessing others is the concept of *chesed*. It's the one and only thing that supersedes the *Shabbat*, or "Sabbath,"—that is, a day of rest, a day to do no work of any kind. The highest form of *chesed* is giving to the poor; it also encompasses helping a neighbor or friend with an important need, whether physical, emotional, or spiritual. *Chesed* is taught in Judaism using the principle that, when you are serving others, you are serving God! It is a form of worship. That's why Jesus says in Matthew 25:40 (author's present tense), "Whatever you [do] for one of the least of these brothers and sisters of mine, you [do] for me." For example, when I meet with and counsel teenagers who can't offer me anything in return, it is an act of loving-kindness—not only to them, but to God Himself!

In John chapter 5, Jesus heals the paralytic at the pool of Bethesda on the Sabbath. This man had been at the pool for thirty-eight years without being healed. Jesus tells him to pick up his mat and go home. The religious leaders were furious when they discovered this—they accused Jesus and the man of breaking the Sabbath (it was unlawful to carry anything, including a mat). However, Jesus didn't break the Sabbath; He was showing loving-kindness. *Chesed* was shown, and it superseded the Sabbath. When Jesus told His followers that, if they love Him, they'd keep His commandments, He was telling them to live out and display the principle of *chesed*.

Our purpose and vision must demonstrate God's priorities—and that includes showing loving-kindness. Otherwise, it's not biblical purpose, and it won't be fulfilling—to us or to those we serve. Jesus made disciples by modeling the principles of the kingdom of God, and leading them in doing the same. This is what biblical purpose is about. Living out biblical purpose will intertwine these two guidelines—the Great Commandment and the Great Commission. Loving others and disciple-making were the two keys to Jesus' purpose; therefore, they must be *our* guiding stars, as well. You can't live out your purpose without these guidelines. Any purpose that doesn't include Jesus' model is incomplete.

So, what is disciple-making? A disciple is a dedicated follower of Jesus—it's someone who desires to model his life after Christ. One of the goals of our lives is to simply walk and live as Jesus did, and teach others how to do the same. According to one of my mentors, Pastor Mike Coleman, disciple-making is about helping others live out Jesus' principles and purposes. This means that biblical vision involves modeling Jesus' practical and spiritual principles in every area of our lives—to include our work and career—for His glory. Everything we do, whether it's feeding kids, clothing the homeless, educating people, providing medical care, helping single moms, or anything else—is all done with the purpose of sharing Christ's love.

If you want to feed people, feed them—and then share the reason why you're doing it. As one of my best friends, Don Campbell, the founder of Feeding Children Everywhere, says, that's the difference between *preaching* the gospel and *sharing* the gospel. Our lifestyle is our greatest evangelism tool, because it's what causes people to ask why we live the way we do. We don't need to preach at them. We simply minister to them and then share the reason why we are doing it. Jesus' model was simply teaching others the scriptures and demonstrating how to apply them when loving people. If you're a business leader, influence people in the workplace by modeling Jesus. If you're a stay-at-home parent, bring these principles into your parenting and home life. As 1 Corinthians 10:31 (BSB) says, "Whatever you do, do it all for the glory of God."

ALIGNMENT DETERMINES ASSIGNMENT

"Our core values determine our choices which determine our destiny."
—Tim Waisanen

I remember an SUV I used to have that kept pulling to the right. In order to make it drive straight, I had to hold the wheel to the left a bit. After a few months, I finally went to get the front end aligned. To my surprise, my tire treads had worn down more on one side because I'd waited so long. I had to buy two new tires! Had I aligned them sooner, I could have made those tires last months longer than they did. Getting your tires aligned helps your car run more smoothly, handle better and more safely, and saves you money. In the same way, aligning your life with God's guidelines for a more purposeful life enhances your life and saves you time, resources, and pain.

As we lead up to writing your purpose statement, it's important to determine with what you want to align your life. The word "alignment" means to be in the proper position, or form a line or arrangement of things in relation to each other. Setting your core values will help you become who you want to be. **The core values you align with determine who you become—and that determines the assignment God will entrust to you.** Your core values steer your life, family, and career. They are the values and principles you hold deep in your heart. They are the "brand"—the nonnegotiables—of your life. Without core values, you'll quickly get out of alignment and veer offtrack, resulting in burnout and directionlessness.

Tony Robbins says, "What you value will determine your level of living. They create a standard that will create more fulfillment, more impact. Core values are beliefs that will guide your decision-making process so you can have a greater quality of life, contribute more to others, and create more fulfillment and impact!"

In this day and age, it's more important than ever to stand for something. The old adage, "If you don't stand for something, you will fall for anything," still rings true. So let me ask you: who do you want to become in the next three, five, or ten years?

Picture the kind of person you want to become. Then ask yourself, *What kind of things does this person do? How did they get there?* It's time now to do those things.

If you want to lose thirty pounds, then follow what other people did to lose thirty pounds. If you want to become a strong leader, then do what strong leaders do. If you want to own your own business, be the best employee you can right now, until God gives you your own business. If you want your own ministry, serve with excellence where you are now. This is the *hard work*. I once told someone, "If you want to preach the gospel around the world, your spiritual life should look like someone who is doing that right now." I asked this individual, "What does your prayer life look like? What does your Bible studying time look like? Don't tell me that you want to be in full-time vocational ministry but that you barely pick up your Bible!" Whoever you want to become, start doing the types of things they do.

Your core values will be reflected in your vision story and purpose statement. For example, two of my core values are the words "purpose" and "relationships." Everything I do is based on purpose-driven actions and building relationships. When I make decisions, I ask myself, "Does this align with my purpose? What relationships will be impacted as a result?"

WHAT ARE YOUR GOALS?

What do you want to accomplish in the next thirty days? The next ninety days? One year from now? Ten years from now? A chiropractor friend of mine told me that it takes ninety days for the cells in our body to completely replace themselves. We have the ability to change at the biological level every ninety days! Over the next ninety days, through making changes, you can begin a new journey and get on the path to which God is calling you!

Practice doesn't make perfect—it makes permanent. What you practice will become a habit—this is what I tell my soccer players. If you want to get out of the rut, it's time to establish new habits. Take a minute to write down the most important things you need to achieve in order to become who you want to be. It's important to create a long-term plan, but you need to also get moving with some small steps right now. When you begin to make progress, it will fuel you to pursue your purpose even more. Again, dream big, but start small. Stop talking and start doing. After you write your vision story and purpose statement, go back and create correspondinggoals. Write down things you want to do within the next thirty days, ninety days, and one year. Make note of who you want to become. It's time to take action.

WHAT DO PURPOSE STATEMENTS AND VISION STORIES LOOK LIKE?

At this point, it's easy to feel overwhelmed by this process. Believe me, I get it—especially after having helped hundreds of kids develop their statements. It's difficult because these statements require you to reach into the core of your soul. That is why I used the well-and-bucket analogy earlier. This book is just the beginning. If you want a guide to help you pull out your deeper purposes, passions, and visions and put them together, our curriculum and video course are for you. We will walk you, step-by-step, through creating your vision story and purpose statement. We believe God has something incredible lying dormant in your destiny, and we want to help awaken purpose within your soul! Sometimes, your purpose statement isn't obvious to you—that's why you need to have someone help you take those steps.

Your vision story and purpose statement (and your goals) will serve as reminders of where God is leading you. I advise you to post them somewhere in your bedroom where you can see them every day. Even when you're down, they can be an encouragement to you to stay the course. In order for your life's vision story and purpose statement to be complete, they must align with God's guidelines, incorporate the way you're uniquely wired as indicated by the Purpose Cross, and reflect your core values. Go ahead; give it a shot. Write out your vision story first, and then shorten it into your more concise purpose statement. Your purpose statement will become your Star of David.

Below are some examples of purpose statements written by young adults that you can read and use as references as you write your own statement. (You can even see how the first one changed from his college days to his mid-twenties!)

NICK, in 2013: "I want to use my gifts of teaching and problem-solving to impact communities and aid those in need by creating and bringing solutions. I also have a passion for training people in the Word, resulting in disciples who make disciples."

NICK, in 2020: *(Nick went from a high schooler questioning his faith to working in real estate development and serving as a high school soccer coach.)* "To use my gift of teaching and problem-solving to impact my soccer players and colleagues. To influence others for the eternal kingdom of God through stewarding real estate and business assets. To utilize my passion for training people and players in the theological nature of the Word and building relationships with them, resulting in disciples who make disciples."

Evan: *(Evan went from a high school soccer player dealing with depression to serving as a youth pastor to hundreds of students.)* "Utilizing my passion for speaking, I want to inspire Christians to stand for their faith—to become a massive army of true soldiers for Christ who take action, enlist in the battle to build the kingdom of God, and expose the world to the truth and freedom in Christ!"

Spencer: *(Spencer went from being a teenager suffering from low self-esteem, suicidal thoughts, and depression to a young adult serving as a business leader and influencer of other women.)* "My purpose is to use my giftings in serving to help reach young adults around the world; to help spark passion to find their identify in Christ and walk out in the power and authority to reach breakthrough; to know the love of Christ and walk out in the truth of God's Word, and follow after His purpose for their lives!"

Danny: *(college student)* "As an attorney, I want to be a voice for those who don't have one—to help stand up for our faith as Christians in a court of law and help those in our society. Through my passions and gift of serving, I desire to meet the spiritual and emotional needs of others in my community and around the world by building them up to walk in the fullness of who God has created them to be and experience His presence."

Chase: *(college student)* "My purpose is to use my talents and passion for technology to have a global impact on my generation; to be a business leader and innovator that demonstrates integrity and values people more than profit; to use every resource God has given me to show the love of Jesus to my peers who are lost, to open their eyes to the truth of the gospel and ultimately, to help them put their faith in Christ."

CREATING YOUR VISION STORY AND PURPOSE STATEMENT

Your vision story and purpose statement should reflect the truth that your reason for existing is to solve a problem in a way that demonstrates God's love for humanity. These two guiding stars will keep you centered on God's priorities. Both should also have an eternal impact—they should be focused on how to impact the culture around you and point others to Jesus, teaching them His ways and building His kingdom. When your life is used to bless and solve problems for others, you are truly living with purpose.

Now is the moment of truth. Go back and look at how you answered some of the questions at the end of the previous chapters. Reflect on your responses and begin to formulate your vision story and purpose statement. How did you respond when asked about your past experiences, life challenges, Purpose Cross elements, and your vision? As you write, keep these questions and your answers in mind. How do your vision story and purpose statement include both the Great Commandment and the Great Commission? How do they reflect your core values? How do they aim toward making an eternal impact that will last after you're gone?

QUESTIONS FOR SELF-REFLECTION

What's so dangerous about leaving out one (or both) of God's guiding stars—the Great Commandment and the Great Commission—as we pursue our purpose?

_____

_____

_____

In your own words, explain how your core values determine your alignment and, ultimately, where you end up.

_____

_____

_____

_____

Take a few moments to write out your vision story and purpose statement. If you'd like more guidance in doing so, check out our study guide and video curriculum, along with other helpful resources, at peopleofpurpose.net. We know this can be overwhelming. That's why we created this resource—to walk you through the process step-by-step, so you don't miss anything.

_____

_____

_____

_____

CHAPTER 10

PROVISION FOR YOUR PURPOSE

Now that you've written your vision story and purpose statement, as well as your core values, I want to end with some essential thoughts that will help to ensure your success in the upcoming battle. Yes—you will face adversity, doubts, and fears regarding God's purpose for your life. However, remember that where God guides, He provides. It's only through His strength and provision that you can fulfill what He has called you to do.

God is the source of all provision. All our needs are met through Him. There are three key areas in which God has made provision for you to live out His purpose (there are more, for sure, but I want to highlight these): people, words, and finances. All three play critical roles in your success. This may be one of the most important chapters yet, so finish strong, apply these principles, and take this battle seriously! They may determine whether or not you will live out your purpose.

As a soccer coach, I always have a game plan for my team. Part of that plan involves understanding our opponents and exposing their weaknesses. However, my main focus is putting my players in the right positions according to their strengths, focusing on a few key tactics to help ensure success, and holding them accountable, both individually and as a team, to the high standard of which they are capable. When you have a game plan, victory is more attainable.

In the same way sports teams have game plans, **God has a game plan for you to put into place as you begin to step towards your newfound purpose.** This book is about giving you the practical game plan that stems from the spiritual principles of purpose. Part of this plan included writing your purpose statement and vision story and setting goals. Now, as we wrap up, we will focus on a few key ways in which God will make provision for your life. At the end of this chapter, I'm going to share one of the greatest personal stories of breakthrough in my life that illustrates these points. I promise that you'll be encouraged and blown away when you realize how God can provide for *your* purpose!

PROVISION #1

The first way God makes provision for your purpose is through people. On the other side of the coin, one of the main destiny destroyers of your future is found in your relationships. I can tell you story after story of young people who were on fire for Jesus, found purpose, but got sidetracked—usually due to a significant other or close friends. People are a key piece in becoming who God has called you to become and accomplishing what He has set before you to fulfill.

Show me your friends, and I'll show you your future. You will become like those with whom you hang out. Who are your closest friends? If they're not focused on and working towards the type of life you want, then you may need to reevaluate how much time you spend with them. If you want to get closer to God and pursue His purpose, you need to consider the type of people you hang out with—whether they are people who have no vision, who just want to party, who sit around gossiping or playing video games all day. Find people who have vision and passions similar to those you have, and hang around them.

As I stepped into the places God called me to enter, I had to let go of the time I spent with many friends who had different focuses and paths. I'd rather spend time with guys who are passionate about God and His purpose—who have big vision. Those are the men who encourage me and provoke me to pursue my dreams simply through their presence. Surround yourself with those who are like-minded. Maybe you need to get plugged into a church—a community of believers you can do life with, fellowship with, and share your dreams and goals with. Maybe you need to join our social media purpose community to stay encouraged and focused on the purpose God has called you to!

Another way God provides provision through people is by giving you mentors and coaches. These are invaluable people to have as you pursue your next season of life. Joshua had Moses, Elisha had Elijah, Timothy had Paul, and the disciples had Jesus. God puts in your path people who have more life experience than you, who can help you improve and excel. They are the individuals who model leadership and life principles to you. My dad always told me, "Son, things are more caught than taught." That phrase has become a motto of mine. I need men in my life who show me the way. While your coach or mentor can't do it for you, they *can* help encourage and push you forward when you feel like quitting. During the dark times, when you're struggling, you'll need someone with whom to be vulnerable, who will hold you accountable.

Who are your mentors and coaches? Are they parents, friends, pastors, business leaders, or even online influencers? If you don't have them, ask God to bring them into your life. Don't be afraid to ask or pursue them, too!

Lastly, we all need people in our lives to whom we give permission to call us out. One of my mentors and friends, Jim Peters, asked me, "Tim, who in your life can tell you no? If you ever get to a place in life where nobody can tell you no, you're on dangerous ground." Who can tell you, "No. You are not going to wear that outfit, go to that party, stay in that relationship, or settle for second best in your life"? These people will be your greatest cheerleaders. They can hold us accountable when we face temptation and adversity, so we don't go off the rails. They also help us stay focused and challenge us when life slaps us in the face, and we want to give up on our dreams. Find friends and mentors who will tell you no and help hold you accountable to your purpose. This will help you in turn say yes to your purpose!

PROVISION #2

A second way God makes provision for us is through our words. The greatest power we possess is in our tongue. Words plant seeds into our present that provide a harvest in our future. When the Bible speaks of words, or the tongue, it is talking about our profession—the way in which we openly declare our beliefs, faith, and opinions. Proverbs 18:21 says, "In the power of the tongue is life and death, and those that love it will eat its fruit." We have the ability to speak either life or death over our lives. Our words will either build us up or tear us down. You will eat the fruit of what you speak. You'll either be filled with a harvest of faith to fulfill your purpose, or with doubt and fear. You decide what words come out of your mouth!

Our words create our world! One of the main ways we're like God is in our ability to speak.

God spoke, and the earth was created. When we speak, things are created. Our speech shapes our emotions, thoughts, and actions. We talk ourselves into things and out of them. Words bring people together or stir up fights. Just watch social media to see their power. Speech is what separates us from other creatures and one of the reasons we have dominion on the earth. Before you jump to conclusions, this is not a "name it and claim it" viewpoint—speaking things doesn't necessarily mean we'll receive them. This is simply a balanced biblical approach to believing and activating in your life what God's Word says, through the power of professing speech.

The key to stepping into your God-given purpose resides in your mouth. What you speak will either prevent or propel you into your purpose. Youth culture is full of gossip, negative speech, and profanity. Much of the default language is empty and void of God. If you allow yourself to engage in this type of language, you'll fall into the trap of speaking, thinking, and acting just like everyone else. This will prevent your purpose. You'll remain in a place of negativity—stuck. So many abort God's plans for their lives unknowingly because of their critical, negative speech.

God has a special purpose for your life; qualifying for it is contingent upon your willingness to line up your words to God's Word. Some of the most powerful scriptures in this area for young people are hidden in 2 Timothy 2. In this chapter, Paul gives a charge to young Timothy, the pastor of the largest church in Ephesus. Paul challenges him not to listen to false teachers or to the ways of the world, but instead to the special purpose God had for him. Paul was calling Timothy to that holy place where he was useful—a place of willingness to do any work the Lord called him to do. If you can follow this advice, you'll be prepared for whatever God calls you to as well.

What qualifies you for this special purpose? And, conversely, what will *prevent* you from stepping into your purpose? Let's take a look at 2 Timothy 2:16 and 20-23:

> *Avoid godless chatter, because those who indulge in it will become more and more ungodly. . . . In a large house there are articles not only of gold and silver, but also of wood and clay; some are for special purposes and some for common use. Those who cleanse themselves from the latter will be instruments for special purposes, made holy, useful to the Master and prepared to do any good work. Flee the evil desires of youth and pursue righteousness, faith, love and peace, along with those who call on the Lord out of a pure heart. Don't have anything to do with foolish and stupid arguments, because you know they produce quarrels.*

In this charge to Timothy, Paul makes a comparison between "special purpose" and "common purpose." Another version calls it "noble purpose." Noble purpose leads to grace and honor, while common purpose leads to dishonor, shame, and disgrace. The path of common purpose is the one most of society takes.

An object with a special purpose is useful, valuable, and profitable for the master's use. This passage contrasts objects of gold or silver with objects of wood and clay. Anything made of wood was porous; over time, it could absorb and contain germs. If a clay object developed a crack, it had to be thrown away. Clay and wood were common. Gold and silver, however, were objects of value and honor. They could be traded for other things of high value. They were washable and reusable—they would last forever.

Stepping into your special purpose involves being purified, like gold and silver. That's what the blood of Jesus does for you and me. However, we have a responsibility to stay clean and separate ourselves from the ways of the world. This happens through our confession—through what comes out of our mouths. The Bible says in Luke 6:45 [NKJV], "Out of the abundance of the heart [the] mouth speaks." What's in your heart will be revealed through your mouth. First John 1:9 also says, "If we confess our sins, he is faithful and just and will forgive us our sins and purify us from all unrighteousness." Confession keeps our hearts clean and purified.

Paul strongly advised Timothy to avoid "godless chatter" or, as another version calls it, "profane and vain babblings," because those who indulge in them become more and more ungodly.

Manifesting this kind of talk is the devil's trap to keep this generation from fulfilling God's purposes. The Greek word used to describe this type of "ungodly" speech is the word *bebelos*, translated as "profane" or "godless." It's where we get our English word "profanity." Profanity means "to walk or take a step." It's also translated as "the trampled places and spots that are open to the casual steps of careless passersby." This carries the idea of something being a place of easy access—ungodly and common. To sum it all up, godless chatter paints a picture of casually walking down ungodly paths. When you follow the same footsteps of the world, you are on the profane path, and therefore live a profane, common purpose.

The word "chatter" comes from the Greek word *kenophonia*, which has two root words: *kenos* and *phone*. *Kenos* means "empty"—the absence of good (and, therefore, contains the presence of evil). *Phone* means "voice, language, sound, tone, or to articulate." When you combine them, the word carries the idea of the battle between the holy and unholy—good and evil—profane and purposeful. Godless chatter represents brainless activity, wasting your time, and doing nothing productive. Lastly, it describes the perverted speech that comes out of our mouths: speech that is twisted, lacks God, and is full of man's wisdom. Godless speech is much broader than negative words—it's void of God altogether!

This simple phrase, "godless chatter," is critical to God's provision for your purpose. That's why I spent time unpacking it. I want it to be clear: Godless chatter is, essentially, walking down ungodly paths of speaking and living—paths that are empty, aimless, useless, and that completely lack anything of God. This is the path of common purpose. However, God has called you to a *special* purpose! When we focus on negative speech, gossip, and destructive criticism, we waste our profession and our purpose.

God is looking for a generation who will crave the things of Him more than the things of culture. Second Timothy also says to flee youthful lust and desires. Youthful desires are the things of the world that have nothing to do with God. These are the cravings and longings for what is forbidden. I believe these can include young people who crave and are obsessed with things like social media, pornography, gossip, comparison games, money, and popularity and, therefore, aren't focused on the things of God. "Fleeing" is an urgent action, not a casual one. Now, I'm not saying you can't play video games, have a boyfriend or girlfriend, enjoy social media, make money or even want to be well-liked. But when you're consumed by and addicted to these cravings, you're no longer pursuing God, but the world. Chasing these things is running away from God. As long as this generation pursues youthful desires, it'll be disqualified from walking in God's special purpose and will settle for the common life of the world.

Provision for our purpose is given to us when we cleanse ourselves from godless chatter. In verse 21 of the above passage, it says, "Those who cleanse themselves will be an instrument for special purposes, made holy, useful to the Master and prepared to do any good work." The word cleanse also means "purge." It is "to turn oneself about for the purpose of avoiding something." This is where we get the concept of repentance. If you want your life to be used to the highest degree by the master, you must cleanse yourself from godless things. You must take responsibility for what you watch, whom you listen to, and what you say. You are the only one who can make the decision to get rid of those negative influences in your life.

Don't compromise your standards. **If you want to step into your destiny and purpose, take the path that's different from the common path of the world.** Avoiding godless chatter and fleeing youthful desires is the formula for passing the test and qualifying for God's special purpose. Instead, let your life and speech be filled with God-talk, consumed with passion for Him. This is the path to receiving the greater call of God on your life.

THE FOUR-HOUR CONVERSATION THAT CHANGED MY LIFE

One day, I met with Rabbi Gary Fernandez for four hours. It forever changed the way in which I speak. Usually, I'm an extremely positive person; however, I was going through a period of time when everything was falling apart financially. I found myself being negative, complaining a lot, and feeling frustrated. Sometimes, I used positive talk, but then negative speech would take over. During our conversation, Gary shared some truths that have shaped my life to this day. During the weeks that followed, my wife even said to me, "Tim, there's something different about you. I can see it and feel it. You're not complaining anymore. You're way more positive. Something has really changed."

Rabbi shared how, Judaism—in which our Christian faith has roots—says to always speak life, not negativity. Once you pray for something, you are to stand in faith—future prayers are to simply thank God for that which we've already requested. This is how you bring things from the spiritual and manifest them in the physical. Rabbinical teaching says negative talk and gossip is designed to kill not only the person about whom you're talking, but also the person who is listening to you! Second Timothy 2:14 says, "Keep reminding God's people of these things. Warn them before God against quarreling about words; it is of no value, and only ruins those who listen." We are not to even *mention* the enemy at all, or give him credit. Too many followers of Christ spend way too much time talking about the negative things—how Satan is beating them up or what he stole from them. The Word of God says in Psalm 113:3, "**From the rising of the sun to the place where it sets, the name of the LORD is to be praised.**" God's praise should always be on our lips. When we are praising Him, we are coming into agreement with Him—lining our lives up with Him. Our words should be focused on what God's Word says, not what the world is doing or how our circumstances make us feel.

Satan's name in Hebrew means "accuser." His job is to condemn us—to make us believe that we can't be close to or worthy of God. He wants to get us into a negative narrative that causes us to accuse others, as well. He wants to fill our mouths with negative words about our situation. If he can do that, he can keep us in bondage. If he keeps you bound up in negative gossip and speech, he can keep you from stepping into your purpose.

THE SILVERSMITH AND THE SILVER

Silver exemplifies the process of us becoming more like our Savior. Preachers and Christian TV shows talk about gold all the time, but nobody seems to talk about silver. In the Bible, silver is symbolic of redemption. Servants were purchased with silver. Jesus was sold for thirty shekels of silver for our redemption. Malachi 3 says that Jesus comes to refine us and make us clean, just like in the process of silver.

Silver has to be worked with the hottest fire there is because it is an extremely hard metal. Gold takes a lower heat, because it is softer. When a silversmith purifies silver, he wears a mask and uses tongs and long gloves. He takes that piece of silver and puts it into the fire. He doesn't take his eyes off the silver. When it gets to the hottest, correct temperature, he takes it out, puts it into the water, and looks at it.

If the silversmith takes his eyes off the silver while it's in the fire, it could get too hot and be destroyed. He knows the exact temperature it needs. Over and over, he inserts the silver into the fire and then douses it into the water, until it is purified.

What is the silversmith looking for? How does he know when the silver is done and fully refined? He knows it is done when he looks at it and sees his own reflection!

Jesus is the silversmith, and we are the silver. Though silver is valuable to begin with, it is molded and purified. Jesus puts us into fires of adversity in order to purify us, to shape us into people who reflect His image. When people look at us, they see Jesus! He wants to make us more like Him so that, when we look at our lives, we don't see the broken-down person we used to be. We don't see the pain, the hurt, the disappointments, or the failures—all we see is Jesus!

How do we know we're reflecting Christ's image? When our words and actions reflect His! When we talk like Him, when our words line up with His words, when our profession reflects His image, we are being a reflection of Him to the world around us.

Your profession brings promotion and provides the way to the next level. The only way you can go to the next level is through your mouth! It's not just praying and fasting that brings you there—it's your confession through the trial. The praying and fasting change you from the inside out so that your profession can change. When your profession changes, God will elevate you in His timing. When our speech and lives reflect His, we have passed the test, and we are ready and qualified to step into the next season of our purpose.

If you're currently walking through a trial, stand strong. Don't dwell on the trial. Don't allow your feelings to take over by venting about the trial. Put your focus on Jesus. He is watching you, and He understands what you are going through. Remember that, **if God has allowed a trial to come into your life, it's so you can go to the next level in Him, and so that you can be ready for the next step.**

PROVISION #3

God is your source; man is a resource. This is a concept that came to me in prayer one day and I have built my ministry on. We cannot look at man as our source. As we said earlier in the chapter, God is the creator and source of all provision; however, He chooses to use people as a resource to provide for our purpose. Luke 6:38 says, "Give, and it will be given to you. A good measure, pressed down, shaken together and running over, will be poured into your lap. For with the measure you use, it will be measured to you." There are people watching your life who have the ability to bless you or open doors for you beyond what you can imagine!

God has practical provision for your purpose. This book isn't just theory. It's not wishful thinking or merely a collection of suggestions. It's literally the behind-the-scenes of my life—what God taught me as I struggled to find His purpose for my life. These are the tested truths I have lived by. God has performed miracle after miracle to assure that I stay on His path for my life! I know God provides for your purpose, because I'm living proof of a faith walk that very few understand. I am now convinced that where He guides, He provides. His vision provides provision.

One of the greatest ways God will reveal Himself is in the way He provides for your purpose in practical ways. Philippians 4:19 (KJV) says, "But my God shall supply all your need according to his riches in glory by Christ Jesus." As I previously shared, Matthew 6:33 (author paraphrase) echoes this truth: Jesus said to seek ye first His kingdom and His righteousness, and all of these things shall be given unto you. I have lived out these principles, and have seen God come through—even in my darkest moments.

I remember going to Walmart one day. My debit card was declined for a purchase of $2.13—one container of baby food. I had two kids in diapers at the time. Money was extremely tight. I'd been doing youth revivals, speaking to kids, flying around the world preaching the gospel. People were even being healed of twenty-year-long debilitating illnesses. Hundreds were coming to know Christ. Yet here I was, almost in foreclosure, ten months behind on the mortgage for my two-bedroom townhouse. I was doing God's work, but I couldn't pay my bills.

During this season, I was the most frustrated and discouraged I'd ever been while in ministry. I wondered where God was. Why had He left me hanging? I remember praying, "God, I've been faithful in serving you. I've been obedient, doing exactly what you called me to do. Why haven't you provided the way I thought you would? Where are you, God? What am I supposed to do? Should I get a job? Should I give up and do something different? My family is my number one ministry, and I'm not taking good care of them right now. Surely, this can't be your will."

During this time, I was under so much emotional stress and spiritual attack that my hands were actually exploding with blisters—it's called dyshidrosis or dyshidrotic eczema. For three years, I lived my life in medical latex gloves and coconut oil. Blisters would form, swell up, and itch like crazy. Sometimes, I'd even squeeze them until they popped because they itched so bad. I'd squeeze the puss out, then itch and rub the area non-stop. After a few days, my hands would dry up and crack. This process repeated itself almost weekly. Blisters formed, itched, dried up, and cracked. Even the slightest movement of my fingers caused the cracks to tear open and bleed. A few times, I even woke up in the morning with blood on my sheets. It was brutal. I felt like I was going to lose my mind. It was incredibly painful to move my hands; that's why I kept them in coconut oil and gloves—to help with the pain.

I went to doctors, dermatologists, nutritionists, and chiropractors, but nothing changed. I thought it was something nutritional, so I even did a forty-day fast, eating just vegetables and fruit. Still nothing. Then, one day, my dyshidrotic eczema cleared up out of nowhere. After three years of dealing with this, and during a time when I was eating unhealthily, it disappeared within a week! God miraculously healed my hands! This condition was caused by stress and fueled by the negative words I continued to speak over my life and situation. About two months after my meeting with Rabbi, the healing finally manifested in my body—around the same time I changed what I was speaking over my life. **I know for a fact that the words I was speaking over my life were transforming me from the inside out.**

One month later, in November of 2013, God brought about the greatest financial miracle that I've ever personally experienced. One of our long-time donors and close friends asked to meet with us. We spent time updating them on the ministry, told them some stories about the youth we were working with, and then gave them gifts. Afterwards, our friends said they had something to give to us, too. They handed us a square, flat object in wrapping paper and instructed us to open it. The wife got out her iPhone and began recording.

I thought, *This must be something special they're showing us or giving us*. Of course, we started trying to guess what it was: "Are you pregnant with your third child? Is it a picture of your family?" They said no.

As we unwrapped it, my wife and I began to weep! It was a picture frame with some writing on it. It read:

The Waisanen Family

Joshua 24:15: "But as for me and my house, we will serve the Lord."

Below the verse was written the address of a house, followed by the date *July 2014*.

You have to understand: I'd mailed newsletters to this same address for several years. I knew this was their home address. I looked up at my friends, who were now also crying. "What?" I asked. "Are you giving us your home?"

"Yes," they responded. "The Lord told us to give it to you. It's debt-free, the mortgage is paid off. God told us that the place you're going and the purpose He's called you to is so big that you have to be free!"

Through my tears, I said all I could think to say: "Wow. Well, this will help!" What a miracle!

This house is a three-bedroom, two-bath home, with an office, a two-car garage, a fenced-in backyard, and a circular front driveway! It was a $230,000 gift, and it had no mortgage! Now, it's worth over $400,000. It's the type of house we'd dreamed of for ten years yet couldn't afford. God gave it to us for free! Not only did this give us a new home to live in and run our ministry out of, it also allowed us to keep our little two-bedroom, 1,000 square foot townhouse as a rental and long-term retirement investment property. Our friends gave us a debt-free house and a rental income for life—all in one day!

I know you may be thinking, *Well, didn't people give this to you?* Yes, but it was because God gave our friends the same dream twice exactly two years apart from each other. She dreamt that dozens of young people were outside trying to break in the house. They weren't trying to steal anything, and they weren't trying to harm the family. They were just desperate for what was in the house symbolically. They knew this represented Karla's and my ministry. They prayed about this decision for two years; then she had the same dream for the second time and knew it was from the Lord. God was the source and reason behind it all. No human would give a friend a house unless God alone inspired them to do so. God is our source; man is the resource!

God has provision for your purpose! Please hear my heart in this. I tell you this extremely personal story not to boast, but simply to show you that **God will provide for where He guides.** I want to encourage you that God has provision for your practical needs. Maybe you're reading this and wondering if you can really trust God. Maybe you're walking through the fire of adversity right now, and asking God how you're going to make it out. Or maybe you're stuck in a job you don't like, believing for something better. God can be trusted. Seriously, I want you to know, beyond anything, that you can trust God with everything, *including* your practical needs. Don't give up. Stay in faith. God will provide for your life and the things He calls you to do. He will reveal Himself—you simply need to be willing to step out in faith and trust Him.

God will supply all your needs. It may not be a house, a building, a new car, or some big check, but He will provide the resources, finances, and open doors you need to accomplish the things He calls you to do. Then again, He may give you something even bigger than you imagine, or open a door that blows your mind. Ephesians 3:20 says He "is able to do immeasurably more than all we ask or imagine." Just maybe, if you step out in faith, God will bless you beyond what you could ever dream.

A FEW CLOSING THOUGHTS

The world lies and says you won't make it. It plants doubt and fear in your head. It tells you you're not good enough or talented enough. It tries to tear you down. God is saying that it's time to rise up and step into the purpose for which you were created! He has made a proposal to you and offered you an abundant life. Stop making excuses, allow God to get you unstuck, and let go of the past and those things that hinder you.

Your identity is being a child of God. You are forgiven, set free by the blood of Jesus, and created to live with purpose. You are good enough and you have value, because Jesus says so. It's time to believe in yourself and believe in the One who breathed life into you. You were made for more—made for relationship with Him—made to solve a problem on this earth. Your life is not about you; it's about Him. Every talent, ability, and gift He has placed inside you is meant to bring glory to His name as you impact your world. All of this is not because of any performance, but because of how good God is. We don't deserve it, but through His grace, we get to play a role in the greatest story of all time.

It is through living in God's presence that His purpose will be birthed in your life. It's by His power that you will accomplish every vision He puts in your heart. You are unique. You are different. There is nobody else just like you. Dare to dream differently than anyone else has, and let God give you a vision to do something nobody has ever done. You don't have to figure it all out right away. Remember, purpose is a lifelong process, not a one-time event. It will grow and evolve over time.

As you follow Him on this faith-filled journey, may His presence be your main desire. From it will flow everything you need to fulfill the reason you exist. Remember that purpose is a person, not a plan. Move forward declaring with your mouth the promises of God over your life and over your destiny. Stay positive when adversity comes. Avoid godless chatter and the common life of the world. Instead, live dedicated to God's special purpose as you stir up the gifts He's deposited inside of you. Stay connected in a faith community, and refuse to settle for second-best. You could have been born at any other time period in history, but God chose you for such a time as this.

Remember, your purpose is not about you, but about surrendering to God's plans for your life—laying your life down for His cause. This is not going to be easy. There will be struggles. However, the apostle Paul said, "I consider my life worth nothing to me; my only aim is to finish the race and complete the task the Lord Jesus has given me—the task of testifying to the good news of God's grace" (Acts 20:24). In his final letter, at the end of his life, he wrote, "I fought the good fight, I have finished the race, I have kept the faith" (2 Timothy 4:7). Only when we have this same mindset will we truly live out our biblical purpose like Paul.

This world is full of people who will leave this earth with unrealized dreams and visions—people who got comfortable and complacent, and never stepped into their God-given purposes. **When I stand before God, I want to hear, "Well done, my good and faithful servant!" How about you?** Take the next step in your journey. I pray that this book is the beginning of a new season in your life. May it be a road map and a catalyst to provoke your dreams, ignite your passion, and awaken your life's purpose!

QUESTIONS FOR SELF-REFLECTION

Think about the top people through whom God has brought provision into your life. Who are they? How have they propelled you toward your purpose?

_____

_____

_____

Do you think this culture underplays or overplays the importance of the spoken word? Explain your answer.

_____

_____

_____

In what ways is God calling you to deviate from the common, worldly path as you pursue His purpose for your life? How is He refining and sanctifying you (setting you apart)?

_____

_____

_____

_____

As you finish this book, make note of the biggest takeaways you've gleaned, as well as any questions or concerns you still have about finding and fulfilling your purpose!

_____

_____

_____

THE GOOD NEWS

"Sin and hell are married unless repentance proclaims its divorce."
—Charles Spurgeon

A few years back, my wife and I went to Israel and toured the Holy Land for twelve days. It was amazing! One lady who was touring with us was an ICU nurse. One day, while talking, I asked her, "Do you have any crazy stories from working in the Intensive Care Unit?"

She said "Oh, yeah, especially since you talk to young people about Jesus and His purpose!" She shared how, a few times, patients had woken up while flat-lining and screamed. One specific twenty-one year old screamed, "I see fire! I see fire—help! They are coming to get me! No, no, nooo!!" Then, *boom* . . . they died.

Don't be fooled. There is a heaven to be won and a hell to be shunned. I am not trying to scare you. I have nothing to gain by whether you choose to believe or not. I just want you to hear some truth that maybe you haven't heard before.

The word "gospel" means good news! Maybe nobody has ever explained the gospel to you. That is why I wrote this section—to simply and clearly share the general theme of the gospel. The gospel is that Jesus came and made a way for people to spend eternity with Him in heaven. At the end, we either accept Him and receive the free gift of salvation, or we don't. The choice is ours. God does not send anyone to hell—one's decision to not receive Jesus does. His Word says it is His will that none should perish! He gave us the gospel, and it's our choice. We have to decide what to believe.

Although I have my beliefs according to Scripture, I am not here to debate theology of a literal and eternal hell. You must come to your own conclusion about what hell may look like. However, what I'm saying is that there's a reason Jesus was willing to endure this punishment in our place. Think for a minute about how brutal, painful, and disgusting the scene of Jesus on the cross must have been! He was naked, bloody, and almost beaten to death. Nails in His hands and feet. A crown of thorns smashed down onto His head. What Jesus went through is a picture of what He is trying to save us from! He could see what was coming to mankind. It had to be something so horrific that it caused Him to willingly sacrifice His body in this manner.

This Jesus is calling you to become a part of the cast of the greatest story ever told: how a loving God saved humanity from eternal separation from Him. He is calling you to a relationship with Him!

I don't want these words to become a block for you. Maybe you're reading this and saying, "I don't know if I even believe in this Jesus stuff." Or maybe you have been turned off by church. What I'm referring to is not about church. It's about knowing Jesus—not the "church Jesus" many churches project, but the true, living Jesus of the Bible. This Jesus is full of love and not hate. This Jesus continues to forgive when we mess up. This Jesus is still healing people today—physically, emotionally and mentally. This Jesus is helping drug addicts and alcoholics become sober. This Jesus is still casting out demons, healing people of anxiety and depression, and giving them hope. This Jesus helps the poor, the broken, and outcasts! This Jesus suffered and died for us, rose from the grave, and conquered sin and death. This Jesus baptized the disciples with the Holy Spirit and sent them into the world to make disciples and live for His mission—not their own. This Jesus now gives us the power to live this life through faith in Him.

It is a popular belief today that there are many different roads or ways that lead to God in heaven: "If I am a good person, I will go to heaven." Unfortunately, that's not what the scriptures say. There is only *one* way to heaven, and that is through a relationship with Jesus Christ. Salvation is a free gift by His grace, and is not based on our performance or good works (Ephesians 2:7-8). **Leonard Ravenhill said, "Jesus didn't come to make bad men good, but to make dead men live!"** It's not about praying a prayer and going back to your old way of living; it's about giving your whole life to Him. He then gives you back the very essence of life, which is His very presence—His Spirit living inside of you. He then shows you the very purpose for your existence!

It's not about what we can do for ourselves, but about what He did for you and me.

Christianity is a lifestyle of purpose and an invitation to be a part of the greatest story ever told.

God created Adam and Eve, and they lived in the Garden of Eden. They were allowed to eat of any tree in the Garden except the Tree of the Knowledge of Good and Evil, because if they did, they would surely die. They disobeyed God, ate of the tree, and sin entered the world. Mankind was now spiritually dead and separated from God. We could no longer be in the presence of a holy God. The only way to bridge that gap and reconcile man back to Himself was for God to send His Son, Jesus Christ, to earth as a sacrifice on our behalf, to die on the cross for the sins of humanity. Jesus rose from the grave, therefore conquering sin and death and restoring us back to our original place of relationship and communion with our Heavenly Father. We were dead in our sins and are now made alive in Christ.

We now have a direct relationship with God the Father through Jesus Christ. All of our sins have been washed away; we have become a new creation in Jesus—spiritually born again—and we have eternal life with Him in heaven. However, we don't wait until then to enjoy those benefits. Our eternal joy and new life begins *now*, on earth!

My dad once said to me, "Son, the greatest question you will ever ask yourself in this life is, 'Who is Jesus Christ?'" How we answer this question will determine everything in our future! It determines how we treat others, how we spend our money, how we use our time, whom we marry, how we raise our kids, how we view life and, ultimately, where we will spend eternity!

When Jesus was talking with His disciples one day, He made a statement in John 14:6: "I am the way and the truth and the life. No one comes to the Father except through me." Jesus did not say that He is *a* way to heaven—He said He is *the* way! Contrary to many other belief systems out there, there is only one way to heaven, and that is through Jesus Christ. Either He was truly the Son of God, or He was the biggest liar who ever walked the face of the earth. He couldn't be a good man, prophet, or teacher if He wasn't the Son of God that He claimed to be. Either Jesus was who He claimed to be, or He wasn't. He didn't say He *had* truth. He said, "I *AM* TRUTH!"

That means, that unless you have Him in your life, you cannot really know or live in truth. He said, "I *AM* LIFE," not that He *had* life. You cannot have true life outside of Him. We do not possess life in and of ourselves. To possess *Him* is to possess life. You may be alive, but you are not living until you encounter Jesus. In order to live lives of peace, direction, and purpose, we must have our lives built upon what is true, which is Jesus, the Person of truth.

Too many people look at Christianity as a bunch of rules—what you can and cannot do. Instead, it's not about religion but about relationship. Religion is man's way of knowing things about God—facts and information—but religion doesn't allow us to *know* God. Many times, I meet people who can spout off scripture from memory, and have a lot of knowledge about God, but their lives are a mess—these are people inside the church and outside the church; they are wealthy, or poor, or homeless. Regardless of who you are, religion merely means having head knowledge. *Relationship* is having heart knowledge—it's about really knowing Him.

Think about your favorite actor, singer, or athlete. What do you know about them? This list probably includes songs they sing, movies they've been in, sports teams they've played on, the number they wear, or position they play. But if you called them on the phone and said, "Hey, this is (your name), what's up?" They would be like "Uh, *who* is this?" Why? Because you know a lot of facts about them, you've formed an opinion of them, but you don't really know them.

However, what if they invited you out to hang at their mansion for the week? You drove their car, swam in their pool, had dinner with them, slept in their guest room, watched movies, etc. Then, the next week, you called them and were like, "Hey! It's (your name)." They would be like "Yo, what's up, (your name)? How are you?" What changed? You now have a relationship with them—a heart knowledge. The same goes with Jesus. Religion is knowing facts about Him—forming an opinion, whether good or bad. Relationship is truly knowing Him. When you get to truly know Jesus, everything changes. You fall in love with Him.

For those who don't know Jesus, I challenge you to open your heart and life to Him. So many people believe in the scientific method but have never applied it to their faith. In essence, you state the question, collect data, form a hypothesis, do an experiment, record data, and draw a conclusion. In regards to faith, many people simply collect data from their own experience or others' experiences; next, they form their hypothesis and then skip down to drawing their conclusion. But they never *test* their hypothesis!

So go ahead: I challenge you to put God to the scientific method. Experiment with Him by going all in. Give your life to Him, and start it by saying this prayer below. Find out if He is real, and if He'll really change your life! For those of you who already know Him, today, He is challenging you to come closer, to grow deeper, to listen more intently to His voice and what He is saying to you specifically. What's the purpose He is calling you to live out?

Salvation Prayer:

Jesus, I come to You today with an open heart. I want to know You—the real Jesus—the One I have been reading about. So today, I make a decision to put my faith and hope in You. I repent of all my sins. Forgive me, Jesus—cleanse me, purify me, and make me like new. I believe that You are the Son of God, that You died on the cross for my sins, and that You rose from the grave and conquered sin and death to give new life to me. Wash away all my fears, my hurts, my pains, and my sorrows.

I ask You to come into my life right now. I surrender my whole life to You. I turn away from my old life. From this day forward, I want to live for You and not myself. I don't want to do this on my own—I want Your Spirit to come live inside of me. I want to experience Your freedom, joy, and peace in my life. I ask You to set me free in Jesus' name! I take authority over those areas of life in which I am in bondage. I break every chain, I expose every lie that I have believed about myself or You, Jesus, and I choose to receive Your truth about who I am: I am Your child.

Today, I am asking for You, the Person of truth, to come live in my life! I give You permission to show me how real You are! I declare my new life in You. I thank You for loving me. Fill me with Your love and Your Spirit right now, in Jesus' name! Amen!

WOW! What do you feel right now? When you opened your eyes, did you feel lighter—like a weight was lifted off? Some describe it as if they felt like they were dreaming; some say it's a surreal, euphoric feeling. This is because you have literally been reborn spiritually. The Bible, in 2 Corinthians 5:17 (author paraphrase), says, "If anyone is in Christ, he is a new creation, old things are passed away, behold all things are made new!" You have become a new creature, a new person. This is the good news of the gospel of Jesus Christ! Welcome to the family of God.

Please find us on social media and send us a message to let us know that you made this decision and what happened in your life!

CPSIA information can be obtained
at www.ICGtesting.com
Printed in the USA
BVHW060443110922
646600BV00005B/19